Moodle 2.5 Multimedia

Quick and easy ways to add multimedia to your Moodle courses

João Pedro Soares Fernandes

PUBLISHING

BIRMINGHAM - MUMBAI

Moodle 2.5 Multimedia

Copyright © 2013 Packt Publishing

First published: May 2009

Second edition: November 2013

Production Reference: 1181113

Published by Packt Publishing Ltd.

Livery Place
35 Livery Street
Birmingham B3 2PB, UK.

ISBN 978-1-78328-147-3

www.packtpub.com

Cover Image by Abhishek Pandey (abhishek.pandey1210@gmail.com)

Credits

Author

João Pedro Soares Fernandes

Reviewers

Saad Faruque

Anna Krassa (kanna)

Bill MacKenty

Danny Wahl

Acquisition Editor

Ashwin Nair

Lead Technical Editor

Ritika Dewani

Technical Editors

Rahul Nair

Amit Ramadas

Project Coordinator

Rahul Dixit

Proofreader

Hardip Sidhu

Indexers

Mehreen Deshmukh

Rekha Nair

Production Coordinator

Adonia Jones

Cover Work

Adonia Jones

About the Author

João Pedro Soares Fernandes is a science teacher from Portugal, who has been working on Moodle since 2004. He has been involved in several Moodle initiatives at school, university, and government levels as a teacher, trainer, course and content developer, manager, consultant, designer, and researcher.

João's main interests range from education to multimedia, the Web, participation, democracy, and human development.

In a single year, he can be seen in several corners of the earth, either working, visiting schools, hiking, or taking photos in mostly non-touristic venues. He also loves music, old cheap cars, farming, cooking, and spending his time in nature.

I would like to thank my family, friends, colleagues, and students for their support through the sometimes-painful process of writing a book while you work, study, and try to have a life. Thanks for all of the ideas and comments, and thanks for the shared experiences that inspired many of the activities in this book. And thanks to all the free software and free content communities for making great tools and resources available to everyone. This one is ours.

About the Reviewers

Saad Faruque has been working as a technology implementer and manager for the past 15 years, with 8 years focused on the education industry. He is presently working as Head of Solution Development at Xeo InfoSoft (`http://xeois.com`), a Bangalore-based company he co-founded. Xeo helps business to implement and manage open source software, for example, Moodle, Alfresco, Zimbra, ORTS, and Nagios with their Service Level Agreements, in their business setup.

You can visit his blog at `http://tektab.com`. If you need help with Moodle or other open source enterprise implementation, he is available at `faruque@gmail.com`.

Anna Krassa (kanna) has a Bachelor's degree in Librarianship and Information Science, but she works mostly as an e-learning consultant. She lives in North Greece (Nea Moudania, Chalkidiki) and she became the first Moodle certified teacher in December 2006. In May 2007, she became a mentor/assessor for the MTC/MCCC candidates, collaborating with HRD New Zealand Moodle Partner, Certification Central Administration. From 2012, Anna became the main mentor/assessor at the MCCC Central Administration.

Anna has also been working with GAC Corporate Academy since 2007, initially as an external facilitator for HRD NZ Moodle Partner, facilitating the Personal and Professional Development courses. In 2012, she joined the academy, and since then, she has been working as a Moodle administrator.

In Greece, she has worked for the E-learning Services department of the Library of University of Macedonia "Telemathea", for the Greek School Network, and as a volunteer with K12 teachers for an e-school called Mathisis. Internationally, besides her collaboration with GCA and HRD, she has set up businesses in Bahrain (GII Academy), Ethiopia (Mekelle University), Canada (Northern Alberta Institute of Technology), and Cyprus (European University of Cyprus).

On a personal level, she is married to Vasilis, and together they have a lovely girl.

Bill MacKenty has been a professional educator for over 10 years. Now as a school administrator focusing on educational technology, Bill has been part of the "ed-tech" scene in it's most formative and nascent years—even now, though many learning organizations do not fully understand how, why, when, and what they should be doing with educational technology.

An avid Linux system administrator and a Moodle admin and user, Bill manages several Noodle instances and loves learning about the Noodle ecosystem.

Danny Wahl is an educational technology consultant and implementation specialist working in the Asia-Pacific region with a particular focus in international schools. He has assisted several schools in one-on-one computing, online, and mobile-learning programs among other things. When not working, he enjoys web development, studying the Bible, and playing 'ukulele.

www.packtpub.com

Support files, eBooks, discount offers and more

You might want to visit www.PacktPub.com for support files and downloads related to your book.

Did you know that Packt offers eBook versions of every book published, with PDF and ePub files available? You can upgrade to the eBook version at www.PacktPub.com and as a print book customer, you are entitled to a discount on the eBook copy. Get in touch with us at service@packtpub.com for more details.

At www.PacktPub.com, you can also read a collection of free technical articles, sign up for a range of free newsletters and receive exclusive discounts and offers on Packt books and eBooks.

http://PacktLib.PacktPub.com

Do you need instant solutions to your IT questions? PacktLib is Packt's online digital book library. Here, you can access, read and search across Packt's entire library of books.

Why Subscribe?

- Fully searchable across every book published by Packt
- Copy and paste, print and bookmark content
- On demand and accessible via web browser

Free Access for Packt account holders

If you have an account with Packt at www.PacktPub.com, you can use this to access PacktLib today and view nine entirely free books. Simply use your login credentials for immediate access.

Table of Contents

Preface

Moodle 2.5 Multimedia provides you with everything you need to include pictures, sound, video, animations, interactive elements, and more in your Moodle courses. You'll develop Moodle courses that you are proud of and that your students enjoy.

This book was written around the design of an online course called *Music for everyday life* using Moodle, where teachers and students will be required to create, share, and discuss multimedia works. Music was chosen as the main theme because besides being fun and horizontal to all cultures, it's a subject that can easily gather contributions from areas such as Science (for example, Waves and Sound), Geography (with instruments from around the world, such as the Ukulele), Languages (music in itself is a language), World History (from medieval music to jazz), or even Social Sciences (the law around creative works). This book was not made for musicians in particular, and one of its main challenges was to reach different educators from different subjects. Music is simply the way to get all of these perspectives working together.

Throughout the book, we will create some dozens of multimedia artifacts that are hopefully relevant, easy-to-do, and as little time-consuming as possible, to develop for us teachers and trainers with busy schedules. And for this, we will use multiple platforms, free software, and web applications.

Better learning is not necessarily a consequence of instruction, so the focus of the proposed activities will be on giving the learner better opportunities to create and share multimedia artifacts, and to dialog about and reflect on these constructions with others. I hope you enjoy it.

What this book covers

Chapter 1, Getting Ready for Multimedia in Moodle, takes a look at the evolution of multimedia, its advantages and uses in teaching and learning, and how these can be used with Moodle. We will also see some of the requirements for using multimedia in Moodle, and configure it accordingly. We will make three simple experiments in a forum with pictures, sound, and video, to see if everything is working as expected while integrating these in Moodle.

Chapter 2, Picture This, deals with images, so we will look at different ways of finding and inserting images in Moodle. We then learn about image editing tasks, commented screenshots, and comic strips. We will also learn how to export presentations as images, adding them to a Moodle lesson, or as an alternative, publishing these presentations in an online service.

Chapter 3, Sound and Music, focuses on tasks for the Moodle integration of sound and music elements. The resources created will make information available in improved ways to students, and will also get them to create audio works, such as soundtracks, slices, remixes, voice recordings, text-to-speech, and podcasts.

Chapter 4, Video, focuses on video production and editing, looking at different ways of using these in Moodle. We will start by looking at places to find free videos online, find ways of downloading videos from online services, extract DVD selections, create photo stories, screencasts, online TVs, and stop motion videos.

Chapter 5, Understanding Web-based Applications and Other Multimedia Forms, focuses on activities that we can do with Moodle and web tools. We will create interactive floor plans, timelines, maps, online presentations, gadgets to represent data, and mind maps.

Chapter 6, Multimedia and Assessments, deals with multimedia elements in quizzes, lessons, and assignments. We will use applications that allow us to create interactive exercises and games that can be easily assessed from and integrated into Moodle, such as crosswords, puzzles, and matching pairs among others. We will look at rubrics as ways of assessing multimedia works in a quick and easy way.

Chapter 7, Synchronous Communication and Interaction, teaches us how to interact with students in Moodle courses in real time by using an online chat and online meeting service. This allows text, audio, and video chat and also a sketchpad, file sharing, recording, and desktop and screen sharing.

Chapter 8, Common Multimedia Issues in Moodle, deals with some common issues on multimedia in Moodle related to copyright, e-safety, referencing sources, and other similar issues. We conclude with some possible modules and plugins to install in Moodle to expand its possibilities and some criteria for selecting web applications for our classes.

What you need for this book

Let's establish as a basic requirement associated with this book the following hardware:

- A consumer digital camera (or a nice smartphone or tablet) that captures videos and photos with 2 megapixels or more

- A webcam with a minimum of 640 x 480 pixels video and photo resolution

- A headset (better than just a microphone because if you have the computer speakers on, there is the risk of feedback)

- A computer with an Internet connection (of course)

It is also assumed that the computer that will be used to perform the tasks presented in the book has a Microsoft (XP or 7), Mac, or GNU/Linux operating system and some minimum requirements, such as more than 1 GB of memory (ideally more than 2 GB), at least one USB port, headphones, a microphone, the respective ports for these, and enough free disk space to install and use the applications suggested in this book (10 GB should be enough).

For the rest of the requirements, free software will do the trick. The required software are:

- Moodle 2.5 (well, can't run away from it)

- A web browser for all the web applications we will be using (for example, Stripgenerator, SlideShare, Animoto, Grooveshark, Voki, PodOmatic, YouTube, KeepVid, Google Hangouts, Google Drive, Floorplanner, Mindomo, Tiki-Toki, Google Maps Engine, Prezi, and Google+ Hangouts on Air)

- GIMP 2.8.4

- Jing 2.6

- VLC 2.0.6

- Audacity 2.0.3

- Microsoft PowerPoint or similar

- Windows Movie Maker 2012

- JellyCam
- Hot Potatoes 6
- JClic

Who this book is for

The book is primarily aimed at teachers and trainers who run professional courses and have experience in the use of Moodle. At the same time, it is not necessary to have an advanced technical background to create multimedia elements, as the tasks will be simple and as little time-consuming as possible, relevant to everyday use.

Conventions

In this book, you will find a number of styles of text that distinguish between different kinds of information. Here are some examples of these styles, and an explanation of their meaning.

Code words in text are shown as follows: "Paste the code after the HTML tag <p>."

New terms and **important words** are shown in bold. Words that you see on the screen, in menus or dialog boxes for example, appear in the text like this: "Click on the **HTML** button to switch to HTML mode."

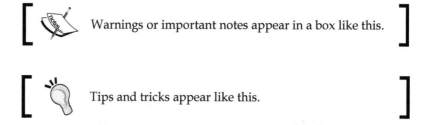

Warnings or important notes appear in a box like this.

Tips and tricks appear like this.

Reader feedback

Feedback from our readers is always welcome. Let us know what you think about this book—what you liked or may have disliked. Reader feedback is important for us to develop titles that you really get the most out of.

To send us general feedback, simply send an e-mail to feedback@packtpub.com, and mention the book title via the subject of your message.

If there is a topic that you have expertise in and you are interested in either writing or contributing to a book, see our author guide on www.packtpub.com/authors.

Customer support

Now that you are the proud owner of a Packt book, we have a number of things to help you to get the most from your purchase.

Errata

Although we have taken every care to ensure the accuracy of our content, mistakes do happen. If you find a mistake in one of our books—maybe a mistake in the text or the code—we would be grateful if you would report this to us. By doing so, you can save other readers from frustration and help us improve subsequent versions of this book. If you find any errata, please report them by visiting http://www.packtpub.com/submit-errata, selecting your book, clicking on the **errata submission form** link, and entering the details of your errata. Once your errata are verified, your submission will be accepted and the errata will be uploaded on our website, or added to any list of existing errata, under the Errata section of that title. Any existing errata can be viewed by selecting your title from http://www.packtpub.com/support.

Piracy

Piracy of copyright material on the Internet is an ongoing problem across all media. At Packt, we take the protection of our copyright and licenses very seriously. If you come across any illegal copies of our works, in any form, on the Internet, please provide us with the location address or website name immediately so that we can pursue a remedy.

Please contact us at copyright@packtpub.com with a link to the suspected pirated material.

We appreciate your help in protecting our authors, and our ability to bring you valuable content.

Questions

You can contact us at questions@packtpub.com if you are having a problem with any aspect of the book, and we will do our best to address it.

1
Getting Ready for Multimedia in Moodle

Multimedia is a very old human endeavor and curiously, it all started with images, more than 30,000 years ago, painted by prehistoric humans on cave walls.

The Chauvet and Lascaux caves in France have some of the oldest paintings known to man.

Source: Sacred destinations (2009). Lascaux cave painting. Retrieved on April 14, 2009 from http://www.sacred-destinations.com/france/lascaux-caves.htm (public domain)

This was the first technology invented to express and capture not only the world we experienced through our senses, but also our imagination and creativity in a medium that could be shared with others.

Compared to these paintings, written text is quite recent, and it marks the beginning of History, more than 9,000 years ago (that's the reason we call the period before it the prehistory). After stone, papyrus was used in ancient Egypt, then parchment, and later paper, invented in China and brought to Europe in the 12th century.

The 19th century saw great developments in multimedia. From photography to motion pictures, from mass production of paper to the new process of printing images and text on the same page, all of it was invented during this time.

Ironically, it took mankind almost all of the 30,000 years since the paintings on cave walls to get a combination of text, image, sound, and video, all working in the same medium. Motion pictures articulating all of these elements were first watched in the 1920s, with soundtracks, subtitles, and of course pictures—still or moving.

The real revolution started with the advent of computers and the Internet, and later on the World Wide Web in the beginning of the 90s, and economically accessible technology for the masses. And finally, after thousands of years of human history, we (not just an elite few) can now create multimedia easily and share it without great effort. In a way, it's a new era for human imagination, creativity, and expression.

This book is about exploring these new possibilities not only for teachers and educators but also for students and learners for teaching, learning, and imagining in new ways. And of course, we will be using Moodle for all of this.

In this chapter we will cover the following topics:

- Knowing a little bit about the history of multimedia
- Understanding some reasons for using multimedia in Moodle
- Attaching a sound file to a Moodle forum post
- Embedding an online video in a Moodle forum post
- Inserting an image in a Moodle forum post
- Choosing an equipment and software to start creating multimedia

Multimedia in Moodle

Moodle was built around an idea of learning what happens when a group of people construct things for one another, collaboratively creating a small culture of shared artifacts with shared meanings (refer to `http://docs.moodle.org/25/en/Philosophy`).

Moodle makes available many resources (web pages, books, files, links, and so on) and activities (forums, assignments, quizzes, lessons, databases, glossaries, and so on) to support teaching and learning, but what can distinguish working with these from paper and pencil work is the way we explore the possibilities of computers and the Web to articulate multimedia elements with text. Creating these multimedia elements, a very powerful concept too, is not possible using Moodle (it is not in its scope either). So when I am talking about using multimedia in Moodle, I am talking about the creation of multimedia using other kinds of tools, later integrated, discussed, and assessed through Moodle.

Using multimedia in this way can provide more opportunities to a group of teachers and students for the construction of, in this case, **multimedia artifacts**. We will try to use multimedia not only as a product for better delivery, but also to improve the ways in which students can construct multimedia artifacts.

It is usually said that multimedia can be beneficial for learning, as it can approach diverse learning styles, add interactivity and learner control, reduce the time required to learn, or extend the information presented through different channels. When we talk about multimedia artifacts, we are talking about content; however, I would say that pedagogy is also important. This is why we should also value diverse classroom practices around multimedia rather than just using it exclusively for delivery.

This book was written around the design of an online course called *Music for everyday life* using Moodle, which is available at `http://www.musicforeverydaylife.net`. This course is open to everyone (no enrolment key is needed; it has a guest access), so you can share it with colleagues as it is licensed under a Creative Commons Attribution license. This gives you a lot of freedom in using and remixing the course's content in your own course.

You might ask, why music? Music, besides being fun and horizontal to all cultures, is a subject that can easily gather contributions from areas such as Science (for example, Waves and Sound), Geography (with instruments from around the world, such as the Ukulele), Languages (music in itself is a language), World History (from medieval music to jazz), or even Social Sciences (the law around creative works). This book was not made for musicians in particular, and one of its main challenges was to reach different educators from different subjects. Music is simply the way to get all of these perspectives working together.

About the course Music for everyday life

As explained before, this book is written around the design of an online course called *Music for everyday life*. The main goal of the course is to develop a basic music literacy that can be used in the daily life of teenagers and adults.

I'm not a professional musician (or a talented amateur) so I'm not expecting the course, *Music for everyday life*, to be the online reference in music education. Music was chosen as the main subject of the course so that it could be meaningful to as many people as possible. As it permeates all areas of life, I have tried to create a curriculum that reflected this, approaching music from a broader perspective and not just basic music theory or instrument playing.

While designing this course, I tried to combine my experience in teaching (mainly science and ICT in education), my time as a student in a Jazz school in Portugal, and all that teenage period that some of us go through when we want to be stars, live somewhere between a studio and a stage, sell CDs, and be famous. Some of my friends who accompanied me during this period are now professional musicians (one graduated in the conservatory of Amsterdam), others changed paths despite their talent and are now business men or designers. I became a science teacher; the studio times are gone, and I really like what I do now. However, music will always be a part of my life, and this course was an opportunity to remember and share it with others.

The course structure

The course Music for everyday life will be organized around 10 modules (adding one presession for preparation and one post-session for follow up), corresponding to three hours of work each, for a total of 30 hours. The course can be used either in distance education or combined with regular classes, what we call blended-learning or b-learning, and it can be used either for a small class or as a **Massive Open Online Course (MOOC)**.

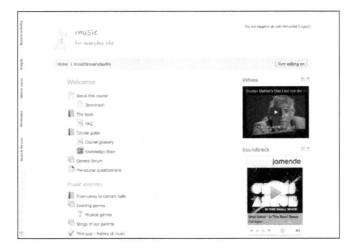

Each of the course's 10 modules will have a standard structure as follows:

- One multimedia resource for content delivery
- Two activities involving the creation of multimedia artifacts (as a group or individually, computer-based, online-based, classroom-based, or out-of-school-based) with informal peer assessment and interaction
- One formal assessment

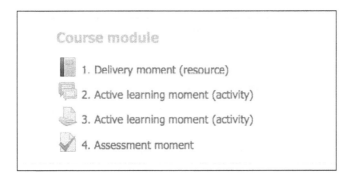

For each module, we will develop multimedia content such as images, audio, video, and interactive content. So in total, we will create some dozens of multimedia artifacts that are hopefully relevant, are easy-to-do, and are as little time-consuming as possible to develop for us teachers and trainers with busy schedules.

The course content

Using multimedia for content delivery and building our own teaching material can be time-consuming, and as we know being a teacher or a trainer is time-consuming just by itself, without the need for any extra workload. This book will focus on simple multimedia elements that you can create or find online without a huge effort, for your everyday life as a teacher or a trainer. Even if you are an enthusiast of digital technologies, keep this in mind: leave time and space for your students or trainees to explore the tools and create multimedia assignments. Don't put all the weight on your side. Better learning is not necessarily a consequence of instruction; so the focus of the course will be on giving the learner better opportunities to create and share multimedia artifacts, and to dialog about and reflect on these constructions with others.

Nowadays, you can find a lot of free content on the Web that can be used for educational purposes without limitations. I would like to thank the authors of this content for their contribution to this culture of sharing we live in now. The same goes for the communities of free software and the companies that provide software for free, for opening up opportunities to many people on which this book and the course are built upon. Building on their work is like standing on the shoulders of giants.

The course modules will be organized around the following themes:

- *Module 1, Music evolves* – dealing with the history of music across the ages and within different genres.

- *Module 2, A world of music* – approaching the cultural diversity and music in different cultures.

- *Module 3, Music and media* – having a critical look at the message underlying music, especially in lyrics and music videos.

- *Module 4, Music as a language* – understanding basic music theory and learning to play an instrument.

- *Module 5, Being a musician* – exploring some daily events in the life of musicians.

- *Module 6, Spaces for music* – looking at music studios and technologies that support musical creation.

- *Module 7, Music and the commons* – understanding the business of music and alternative ways of licensing and distributing it.

- *Module 8, The science of music* – having a look at music from a science perspective, mainly sound and waves.

- *Module 9, Music, dance, and emotion* – exploring the links between music, dance, and emotions.
- *Module 10, What's good music?* – reflecting on quality criteria for music.

Prerequisites

Some assumptions are made as the prerequisites both for this book and for the course. These have to deal with knowledge, hardware, and software that will be required to complete all of the proposed tasks.

Knowledge

The course was designed for students who are music beginners and who probably have an instrument, such as a piano or guitar. This is not a necessity, as there will be tasks for students to create music using a computer. Students should also have an intermediate knowledge of how to use a computer, the Web, and Moodle from a student's perspective. This means that students are expected to already know how to manage files and folders, use a digital camera, download photos and videos to a computer, how to install, uninstall, open, and close programs, and so on.

The prerequisites for you, the reader, are more or less the same (you don't need to play an instrument though!), with the only difference being to know how to use Moodle from a teacher's perspective. This means that you should know how to create and configure resources and activities in general, upload files, use Moodle's HTML editor at least for text formatting, manage users, run a simple course with forums, assignments, and basic quizzes (not, of course, for absolute novices in Moodle – there are some nice books from Packt Publishing if you need to improve your skills, such as *Moodle 2.0 Course Conversion* by *Ian Wild* and *Moodle Teaching Techniques* by *William Rice*). If you are thinking that this is too much and that technologies for multimedia creation are far too complicated for you or for your "older" students, have a look at this video http://www.youtube.com/watch?v=pQHX-SjgQvQ from the show *Øystein og jeg* on **Norwegian Broadcasting** (**NRK**) about a medieval helpdesk and this new technology called "book". I usually show it when the "age" argument comes up, and with it the usual assumption that older people can't learn a new technology. They can – it's just a matter of time and attitude.

Hardware

If you are on a tight budget, this is not a limitation for creating multimedia. It's easy to get a digital camera that, in addition to taking photos, also records videos, or to find a cheap headset that can be used to produce some sound, and all of this for less than €100/£90/USD $120.

A low-budget equipment kit

Digital cameras are now widespread and are an interesting replacement for a regular camera. They allow us to create pictures (and most of them allow the recording of videos as well) that can be archived to a computer, USB disk, or the Web. These days, even a regular smartphone has a camera, so this can also be an option. You can also find cheap webcams and headsets.

Let's establish a basic requirement associated with this book and with the participation, as a student, in the course in Moodle:

- A consumer digital camera that captures videos and photos with 2 megapixels or more
- A webcam with a minimum of 640 x 480 pixels video and photo resolution
- A headset (better than just a microphone because if you have the computer speakers on, there is the risk of feedback)
- A computer with an Internet connection (of course)

It is also assumed that the computer that will be used to perform the tasks of the course (and this book) has a Microsoft Windows (XP or 7), Mac, or GNU/Linux operating system, and some minimum requirements, such as more than 1 GB of memory (ideally more than 2 GB), at least one USB port, headphones, a microphone, the respective ports for these, and enough free disk space to install and use the applications suggested in this book (10 GB should be enough).

For the rest of the requirements, free software will do the trick.

Software

Throughout the course we will be using as much cross-platform, free, open source software as possible. This of course, includes Moodle. However, in a few cases, the only Microsoft-compatible software will be the single choice (around three tasks will use Windows-only software) due to the lack of adequate alternatives on other OSs, or its broader distribution (this distribution will probably also apply to the readers of this book). Either way, as we will focus on processes and tasks that are standard, I expect that these will also be useful, no matter which platform you use. Similar software for other platforms will be referred to as well.

Picking up software for multimedia production is very easy nowadays, as many options are available for every need. Another challenge for this book is to select the ones with simpler interfaces that are as multi-platform as possible, and of course, that are free. Sometimes, it will not be possible to get completely cross-platform software (software that can run in GNU/Linux, Mac OS, and Microsoft Windows), but such cases will be rare. The reason for selecting free software as far as possible is that it reduces the barriers to installation on schools' computers and students' personal computers (licenses for this kind of use are generally very open and usually free), so we can invest our money in equipment and time, instead.

As we go along building the course in the following chapters, other tools will be introduced. It's overwhelming if you get a list of more than 20 applications to install at the beginning of the book, so we will introduce new tools as they are needed. Using many tools and strategies and lots of multimedia is not necessarily good, so the proposed tools will always have a context where they make sense, and can be used not only for improved delivery but also for designing activities that are expected to motivate, engage, and create better opportunities for learning.

Configuring Moodle for multimedia

Moodle, as a Web-based learning management system/virtual learning environment, is prepared for a range of multimedia elements (not for creation, but for integration). We can easily add images, videos, and sound files. And if everything works out as expected, we will just need to make a link to the multimedia file, and Moodle will do the rest to embed a player and show it.

However, there are some Moodle settings that we should be aware of that make this use of multimedia easier. We should ask our Moodle administrator to do the following:

- **Enable the multimedia plugins**: In the **Site administration** block, go to **Plugins | Filters | Manage filters** and on the dropdown of the **Active?** column for **Multimedia plugins**, change it to **On** and only apply it to **Content**).

- **Allow the EMBED and OBJECT tags**: In the **Site administration** block, go to **Security | Site policies** and select the checkbox for **Allow EMBED and OBJECT tags** field, and save the changes.

- **Enable trusted content**: In the **Site administration** block, go to **Users | Permissions | Define roles**, and for the **Student** role, select the checkbox **Allow** for the option **Trust submitted content**.

- **Use the TinyMCE HTML editor**: In the **Site administration** block, go to **Plugins | Text editors | Manage editors** and enable it. This option is usually enabled by default.

- **Enable RSS feeds**: In the **Site administration** block, go to **Advanced features** and select the **Enable RSS fields** checkbox. After this, you will need to enable RSS feeds in each module that generates them: **Database**, **Forum**, and **Glossary**. In the Site administration block, go to **Plugins | Activity modules** and select the option **Yes** for **Enable RSS feeds**, after clicking on the name of each of these modules.

- **Increase the maximum upload file size**: Multimedia files can be sometimes larger than common document files, so having a good upload size limit will be helpful. A maximum upload size of 16 MB will be enough for common uses. If our Moodle installation has less than that, we could ask our administrator to increase it. In the `php.ini` file (or in the `.htaccess` file), change the following values: `post_max_size = 16777216` and `upload_max_filesize = 16777216`. In Apache's `http.conf` or `php.conf` file, change the value of `LimitRequestBody` to `16777216`. Then, in the **Site administration** block, go to **Security | Site policies** and in the drop-down box for the **Maximum uploaded file size** field, select **Server limit**.

Note that Moodle administrators can refuse to change some of these settings as they can overload the server, so we may need to ask them to upload larger files for us. Multimedia files, especially videos, can be very large files, so we should have some preoccupation with the size of the files we upload. An alternative that we will explore in this book is to host our files on online services and then link or embed (a concept we will see in a moment) these in Moodle. This will save server space for our school or institution, but can raise other questions such as blocked websites, bandwidth, or e-safety that we will see in this book. Another alternative is to use file formats that have good size/quality ratios, and we will learn how to select and use such file formats later on.

Three simple things using Moodle and multimedia

After going through these steps, it's a good time to try it out to see if everything is working. Let's start with three simple tasks, involving an image, a sound, and a video on a forum, respectively.

Task 1 – adding images to forums

1. Go to the **Flickr Creative Commons** (**CC**) licensed content at `http://www.flickr.com/creativecommons/by-2.0` and search for a photo under an Attribution license (when an image is termed as CC attribution it means that we can use these images without many restrictions, except for citing the author. We will have a look at copyright issues in *Chapter 8, Common Multimedia Issues in Moodle*).

2. On the results page, choose an image. Next, right-click on the image (if you are a Mac user and have a one-button mouse, click on it while pressing the *control* key on the keyboard), choose a size and save the picture to your computer.

3. Finally, upload the image as an attachment to a new forum post, citing the source.

You should be able to see a screenshot similar to the following:

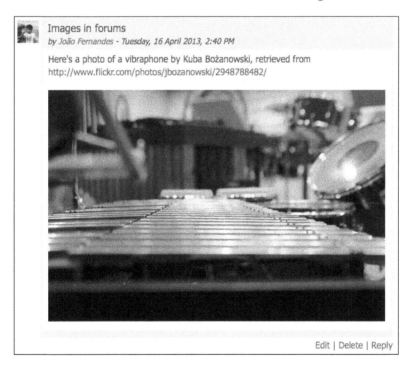

In this case, Moodle has automatically inserted the image for us. It has a width that will fit well in the screen. Sometimes, when the image has a width above say, 800 or 1024 pixels (depending on the monitor on which it is displayed), we will have to resize it, preferably before we upload it to Moodle. You don't have to worry about that for now.

Examples of uses of a forum with pictures

Pictures are sometimes better than a thousand words. We can use them in specific cases of the forum to do the following:

- Sharing photos and report study visits
- Sharing and discussing a painting, a drawing, or a cartoon
- Creating a collaborative photo story, where each post is an element of the story
- Sharing screen captures of works made with software

Task 2 – adding sound to forums

1. Select a song from the WIRED CD (`http://creativecommons.org/wired`).
2. Download it to your computer, again by right-clicking on the link to the music (or by pressing the *control* key plus the mouse button for Mac users), and saving the target of the link to your computer.
3. Write a forum post in Moodle citing the source of the music (never forget the sources—the license of the music of this CD allows noncommercial sharing).
4. Upload the sound file as an attachment on the forum post.

 If you get an error in the upload, the problem may be related to the maximum upload size, site-wide or course-wide. Check your settings.

If everything works as expected you should see a screen similar to the following:

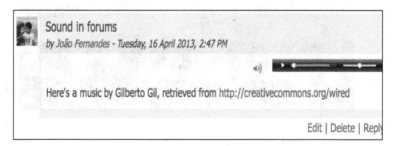

Moodle's multimedia plugin is automatically inserting a flash player for our MP3 file. The multimedia plugin processes the page, looking for links to multimedia files, and when it finds one, it tries to insert a player.

In the case of MP3 files, we should ensure that we have the flash player plugin installed on our browser. We can go to http://www.adobe.com/software/flash/about/ and check this (if we don't have the flash player installed, that's not a problem). The flash player allows the playing of multimedia content, such as audio, video, or animations inside browsers.

We should also have the necessary players for file formats such as MPEG-4 (the *.mp4 files) and Windows Media Video (the *.wmv files) installed on our computer and working inside our browser; for example, a QuickTime player, available at http://www.apple.com/quicktime/download/.

Examples of uses of a forum with sound attachments

There are many uses of audio in other Moodle activities (such as the quiz or the assignment), but we'll just focus on the forum for now. We could do the following:

- Sharing an interview or comment, and vote and comment on it
- Making a class selection of music themes
- Doing a role-play activity in which each student plays a character
- Asking for a poetry selection and declamation by students
- Starting a collaborative and iterative composition of a musical theme, where each new post builds on the one before
- Generating a podcast through the conversion of the forum's RSS feed
- Hosting a Q&A session between the teacher, invited experts, and students
- Using a text-to-speech tool to create fictitious dialogs
- Doing some ear training exercises
- Doing a show-and-tell exercise

Task 3 – adding videos to forums

1. Go to TED (http://www.ted.com/) and search for a video. In the results page, choose one and click on it.
2. Click on the **Embed** button below the video.
3. Copy the code in the form next to **Embed this video**.

4. Open a new forum post and write something about it. Do not forget to mention the source of the video.

5. In the HTML editor, use the *Enter* key after the source and then click on the **HTML** button to switch to HTML mode.

6. Paste the code after the HTML tag <p> (which corresponds to a paragraph in the text), as shown in the following screenshot:

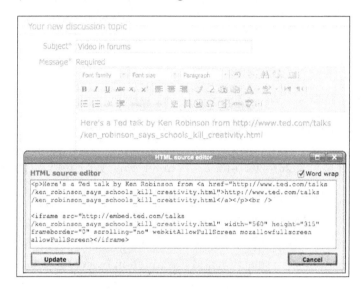

7. Post your message, and the result will look similar to the following screenshot:

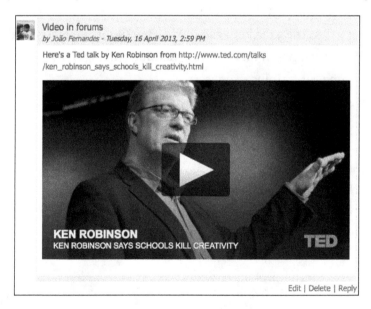

This embed procedure is very helpful, and you should keep these very simple steps in mind:

1. Copy the embed code.
2. Click on the **HTML** button in the HTML editor.
3. Paste the embed code.

In a post, the size of the video (width and height) will fit well in the screen. However, if we were embedding it in a Moodle block, we would have to change something in the code used as is. We will leave that for later, when it's needed.

Examples of uses of a forum with videos

Using forums with videos is a great way to start a discussion, and it can also be used to do the following:

- Commenting on a video excerpt
- Creating a collaborative video selection
- Broadcasting a live event
- Posting a video to add subtitles and comments
- Posting a silent video for students to submit a soundtrack
- Posting a video tutorial capturing procedures for a software application

We have just tried three simple examples of using content that was not made by us. Creating our own multimedia content is another story; however, nowadays it can be quite easy, with the price of equipment going down, software interfaces getting simpler to use, and a wide variety of free software being available for multimedia editing. We now don't have any excuses for not using it, except for a lack of time. The subsequent chapters in this book will deal with this multimedia production, explaining and showing how to create these resources for delivery and active learning, not just as products but also as activities for your students to participate in.

To give you just a flavor of what the course will be, here is a list of some examples that will be developed either for the course by the teachers, or during the course activities by the students:

- Adding short audio clips and voice recordings to forums
- Producing video tutorials explaining some tasks in music software and exploring some websites
- Adding a soundtrack and remixing a video

- Creating an interactive timeline of the history of music
- Creating a collective world map with multimedia placemarks of world instruments
- Designing a music studio floor plan
- Drawing a cartoon strip about a scene in the life of a musician
- Creating a collaborative multimedia music styles glossary
- Creating interactive diagrams and charts
- Using multimedia Moodle quizzes, lessons, and assignments with multimedia, and many other such exciting activities

Summary

We have had an overview of the evolution of multimedia, considering some of the potential advantages of its uses in teaching and learning. These uses can be aligned with the underlying learning philosophy of Moodle, focusing not just on delivery but also on active learning, where students will use the tools for multimedia creation to augment their possibilities to construct, share, dialog with, and reflect upon those constructions with others.

We also considered the basic knowledge, equipment, and software required to start creating our course, *Music for everyday life*, which will gather contributions from History, Geography, Social Sciences, Science, and other fields of human knowledge. And finally, we saw some of the requirements for using multimedia in Moodle, and made three simple experiments on a forum, with pictures, sound, and video to see if everything was working as expected.

So, let's start, just like the Chauvet and Lascaux caves, with images! In the next chapter, we will look at images, learning how to find free pictures for our multimedia projects, edit photos, capture and comment screenshots, and create comic strips and slideshows.

2
Picture This

This chapter will essentially focus on creating and editing pictures for the course *Music for everyday life*, which includes finding free pictures online, making photo collages, and comic strips, or just simple screenshots and slideshows. We will also have a look at some basic photography concepts so that we can start creating and enhancing some nice photos for our course.

By the end of this chapter you will be able to do the following:

- Finding free pictures in online repositories
- Integrating images in Moodle
- Selecting appropriate image formats according to your needs
- Using a set of free software tools for common procedures in picture editing
- Creating and editing photos for the course
- Creating screenshots with comments
- Creating comic strips
- Exporting presentations' slides as images and include these in Moodle lessons
- Publishing presentations in an online service and embedding these in Moodle resources or activities
- Creating photo slideshows

Finding free pictures online

Reinventing the wheel, especially for teachers, is a great path to burnout. Creating pictures for our courses (photos, drawings, and icons), if we are working from scratch, is extremely time-consuming, adding to the course design effort, the interaction with students, or worse, assessment. Fortunately, we are not working alone anymore, as there are many places on the Web where, with the help of millions, we can get ready-made pictures, for free (well, sometimes searching for a nice picture can take a while, but it can be worth the effort!). But first, let's take a look at the basic image formats before we go on to see the places where we can find free online pictures.

The basics of image formats

There are some things that we should know about image formats, particularly how to choose the best formats for our Moodle courses. There are many formats around, but the good news is that we will just need to use three of these in our daily life:

- **GIF**: It's an old format that only uses 256 colors, so it can be useful for storing simple images with few colors, such as logos or diagrams. This format also supports animation (animated GIFs). Avoid it while storing more complex pictures such as photos of landscapes.

- **PNG**: It's an enhancement to the GIF format, supporting 16 million colors, and was created as an open source alternative to GIF. It's a good format for storing images that are being edited.

- **JPEG**: A very common format on the Web and for digital cameras. It has a good quality/file size balance, so if we need to save on space this can be a good format to choose, as it uses image compression. However, if we use this format while editing images (repeatedly saving each time we make any changes to it), we will lose image quality. So to avoid this, while editing, use other formats such as PNG. When you want to publish it on the Web or just send it by e-mail, go for JPEG. The file extension is JPG.

Sometimes it's not just about image formats. For example, we can have huge JPEG files captured in digital cameras with 12 megapixels. In this case, scaling the image to smaller sizes (that will fit well in a screen, if we are talking about using them in Moodle) is the way to go. We will see how to scale images and convert them in any of these three image formats in this chapter.

Flickr

Flickr (`http://www.flickr.com`) is a great online service for organizing, publishing, and sharing photos (or screenshots) and for meeting people with the same interests. It has millions and millions of photos, including Creative Commons licensed photos, as we saw earlier. Among many other things, it allows you to organize photos in sets, edit them, create slideshows, and even overlay photos in an online map. In the Creative Commons section of Flickr (`http://flickr.com/creativecommons`), we can get millions of pictures licensed under Creative Commons licenses, meaning that we can use them in general for educational purposes without major limitations (especially with the Attribution-only licenses). To learn more about these licenses, check *Chapter 8, Common Multimedia Issues in Moodle*, in this book or read the brief explanations in Flickr about them, shown on the right in the following screenshot. We will talk a lot about these licenses as we move ahead with the book.

To search for pictures, we must first click on the **See more** link for the type of licensed photos that we want to use (there is a brief description of the available licenses on the right-hand side of the screen, and also in *Chapter 8, Common Multimedia Issues in Moodle*).

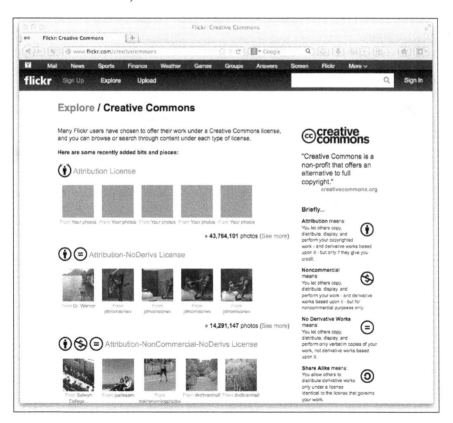

Then, we just need to use the search form available at the top of the page, typing the keywords that we are looking for.

Once we are on the results page, we can click on one of the search results. We will just need to perform the following steps:

1. Right-click on the picture.
2. Click on one of the **Medium** links as shown in the following screenshot (medium sizes generally fit better in Moodle forums and content for most displays; we'll check this later in this chapter).

3. Save the picture displayed in the web browser to our computer.

Just a reminder on how to save a picture from the Web to our computer, here is the basic procedure:

1. Right-click on (or hold the *control* key and click if you're a Mac user) the picture displayed in the web browser.
2. From the menu that appears, select the **Save image as...** option.
3. Select a destination on your computer and save the image to that location.

Every time we save a picture, we must not forget to register some details about it, to properly reference it later in our Moodle course (author, date, page title, picture title, link). Refer to *Chapter 8, Common Multimedia Issues in Moodle*, for more details on referencing sources.

Because the Web is not just about taking but also about giving, next we will see how to upload our own photos to this service, so that others can build on our work too.

Uploading photos to Flickr

The approach we will mainly use in this chapter with regard to pictures in Moodle is to upload images to our course, either to the course's files or as an attachment in several activities. However, if we want to participate in a broader community of sharing (not just in our small course), a solution would be to post the pictures on Flickr, where they will be available to many people, and will constitute a kind of repository of images that we can use in several Moodle courses. But it's not just about sharing or making management easy. It's also about getting feedback from others, contacting the real world, and engaging in conversations about our work. This is a huge opportunity (with risks, if we are talking about students posting their photos, refer to *Chapter 8, Common Multimedia Issues in Moodle*, for a discussion about these concerns on safety) for learning, and a way of participating in the community.

In addition to the web interface, there is also an official picture uploader, the Flickr Uploadr (go to `http://www.flickr.com/tools/`). We will use the web interface though, to create our first picture set.

1. After creating an account, sign in to Flickr.
2. Click on the **Upload** link on the top bar.
3. Drag-and-drop pictures from our computer to the active area inside our browser (we can upload 1 TB of data for free!).

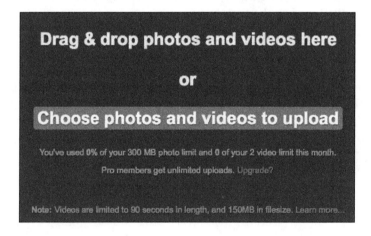

4. Select the pictures you want to add to a set. Use the *Ctrl* key (or the *command* key on a Mac) to select different pictures.

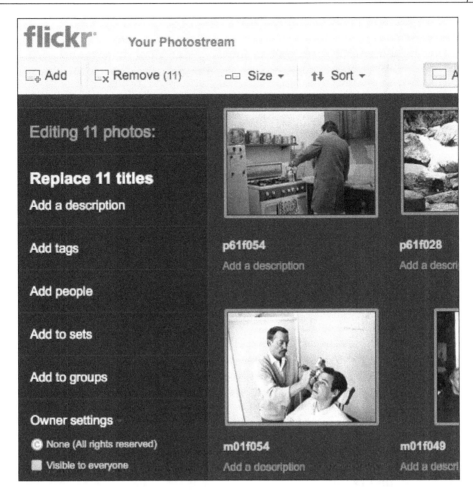

5. Click on **Add to sets** on the left menu and fill in the **Set title:** and **Set description:** fields.

6.   Click on the **Create set** button and we're done!

After we have the pictures online, we can insert them into our course by using the HTML editor, in this case, adding the URL to the photo in Flickr instead of uploading the image to Moodle. However, the photo has to link back to the photo page as this is required by the terms of service of Flickr. We can do this easily by adding the link to that page below the picture, again using the HTML editor.

License

In the account preferences, concerning the license of the photos that we put online on Flickr (`http://www.flickr.com/account/prefs/license`), we can associate them automatically (with the possibility of changing it at any time) to a Creative Commons license of our choice. This can also be done by using a batch edit. This batch editing (`http://www.flickr.com/photos/organize`) allows the control of permissions and even editing (for example, making some photos private, others all rights reserved, rotating, and so on).

Wikimedia Commons

Wikimedia Commons (`http://commons.wikimedia.org`) is a project by the Wikimedia foundation, the same one that is responsible for Wikipedia. Wikimedia Commons hosts all the pictures and other multimedia elements (audio, video, and vectors) included in the well-known Wikipedia online encyclopedia articles. We can find interesting pictures on a variety of topics (using the search form on the left-most side of the screen), mainly under GNU free documentation and Creative Commons licenses, so we can use these without many limitations in our courses.

Other picture sites

In addition to these two services, we can find many other online services where we can obtain pictures, such as:

- **Stock.XCHNG** (http://www.sxc.hu) – an online service where we can download as many pictures as we want, for free
- **Openclipart** (http://openclipart.org) – an online community where we can download and upload cliparts for free
- **Picasa** (http://picasa.google.com) – an online service from Google that allows us to organize our photos

In the course, I have used several pictures from these sources to create course content; for example, in *Module 7, Music and the commons*, I have used the image shown in the following screenshot:

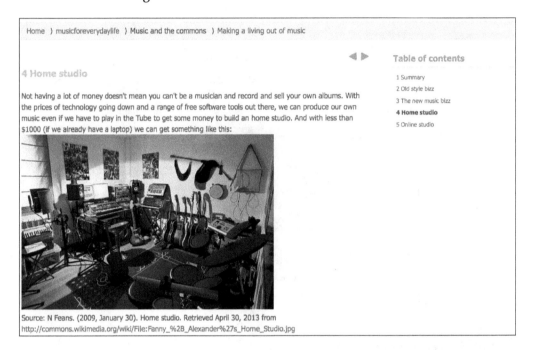

Moodle it!

Inserting images in Moodle is really easy. Now that we have a source of free pictures for our course, there are several ways to insert them, depending on the type of resource or activity that we are using. We will have a look at the following three ways in this book:

- Uploading images as attachments (for example, in forums, glossaries, or databases).
- Using the built-in HTML editor and the course file picker to store the images.
- Embedding HTML code (specific for images) on web forms (don't be scared, it is easy and can be helpful on some occasions, just as we saw with YouTube videos). We will use it later in *Chapter 5, Understanding Web-based Applications and Other Multimedia Forms*, for adding pictures to Google Maps, for example.

For now, let's' just look at the first two ways of inserting images.

Uploading images as attachments

Using attachments is the easiest way to add a picture to Moodle. This possibility is available for some activities in Moodle, such as the forum, glossary, and database, and it's the easiest way for students to submit their pictures to a course. We saw in *Chapter 1, Getting Ready for Multimedia in Moodle,* how we could do this in a forum. Basically, this is the same process of adding an attachment to an e-mail, but in this case, Moodle does the rest to display the image on the forum post (it generates the HTML code needed for this). There is just one thing to keep in mind; when we add a picture as an attachment, it will be displayed in its original size at the end of the text. This means that if our image is too large for the screen size we are using, we will have a problem in visualizing it. In a moment we will see how to resize a picture to make it fit well for our course.

In the glossaries in the encyclopedia display format, images added as attachments are shown inline. In *Module 1, Music evolves,* students are required to add a course glossary about an artist their parents like, with one photo and a music track. While adding an entry, we have a field to insert an attachment.

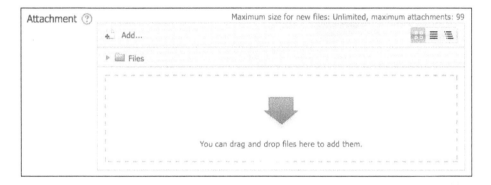

When we save the entry, we will have a glossary entry something like this:

Zeca Afonso

by João Fernandes - Tuesday, 30 April 2013, 2:17 PM

Zeca Afonso was born in 1929 in Aveiro, Portugal, and was one of the most influential folk and political musicians in Portuguese history. One of his musics, Grândola Vila Morena, previously banned, was selected by militars from the MFA (Movimento das Forças Armadas) as a coutersign for the Carnation revolution in April 25, 1974 in Portugal, where the Estado Novo regime was overthrown in a nearly-bloodless military coup. At 12:15AM it was played in the radio show in Rádio Renascença, the signal to take over strategic points of power in the country. At 7.30pm of the same day, President Marcelo Caetano surrendered.

Using Moodle's text editor

Using Moodle's built-in text editor and the file picker is a simple way of inserting images in Moodle, in side blocks, or in any kind of resource or activity. The basic procedure for doing this is as follows:

1. Click on the Insert Image button.
2. Click on **Find or upload and image....**
3. Use File picker to select and existing image or upload a new one.
4. After selecting the file, it will appear in the **Preview** window.
5. Add an image description.
6. Click on the **Insert/update** button.

When we create content in Moodle, by default, we have access to a word processor-like toolbar that helps us format text in what is called a **WYSIWYG (What You See Is What You Get)** interface. In this kind of interface, we can see how the content will look as we make the changes (refer to the following screenshot).

Many of the buttons of this toolbar are fairly standard, but there are some that are not so familiar. However, all software toolbars show hints about the buttons if we hover the mouse over the buttons. This will help us know their functions and will be very useful during the course of this book. In the preceding screenshot, the little button representing a framed landscape in the toolbar's second row shows its function when the mouse is over it (no need to click!), that is, Insert/edit Image.

After we click on this button, the following window appears:

This is the general tab for the standard window for uploading images to Moodle. We can see the image URL, the image description, and a preview of the image. But these fields will be empty because we haven't uploaded anything yet.

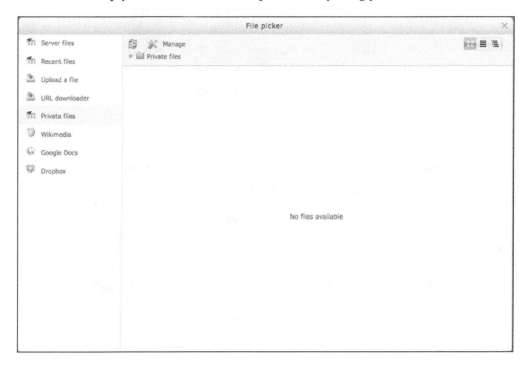

So now, after clicking on the **Find or upload an image...** button, we can pick files from several sources, in this case our **Private files** section, the place where we will upload our images. We will upload a photo of a paleolithic flute to the book *From caves to concert halls* in *Module 1, Music evolves*, to a folder corresponding to this module, in a subfolder just for pictures. For this, perform the following steps:

1. Click on the **Manage** link on the top menu of the File picker. A new window will open.

2. Click on the destination folder in the file picker box (in this case, the previously created images folder where all of the modules' images will be stored).

3. Drag-and-drop the picture from our computer onto the active area.

4. The file will be uploaded to our **Private files** area.

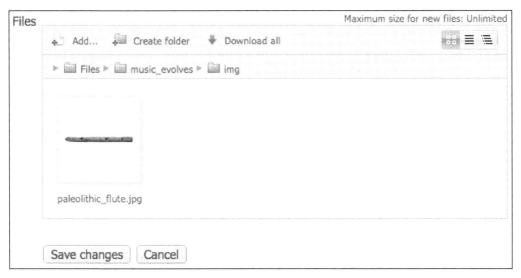

After we click on the **Save changes** button, a thumbnail of the picture will show up.

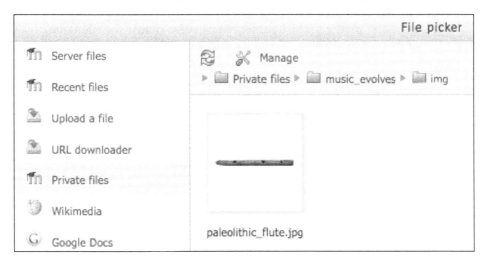

We can now close this window, click on the Refresh icon on top menu of the File picker and finally on the picture thumbnail. After this, we get a new window, something like this:

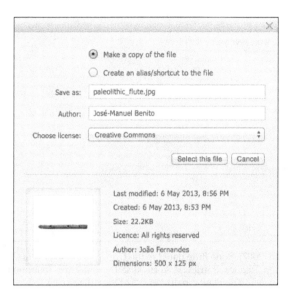

We can now make a copy of the file from our **Private files** area to the course. This is safer as we create an alias and delete this file from our private files, and then we'll end up with a missing image in the course. We can also define the filename, insert the author, and the picture license. Now, we just have to select this file by clicking on **Select this file** and the **Insert/edit Image** window will show up, this time with the image URL and preview of the picture.

Now, something important. In the **Insert/edit Image** window, in the **Appearance** tab, we can resize the picture by changing the width or height dimensions while constraining its proportions. I wouldn't recommend this, as the image may lose quality. The best thing to do is to resize the image in an image editing software application and then upload it to our course, as we will see later in this chapter. You can see some reference values for image sizes in Moodle in this chapter when we talk about resizing procedures.

Finally, in the **General** tab, we can add **Image description** (a matter of accessibility, useful for screen readers), click on the **Insert** button, and then our book will look something like the following:

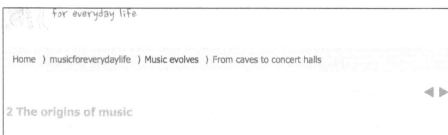

Home 〉 musicforeverydaylife 〉 Music evolves 〉 From caves to concert halls

◀ ▶

2 The origins of music

The origin of music is not known as it occurred prior to the advent of recorded history. Some suggest that the origin of music likely stems from naturally occurring sounds and rhythms. Human music may echo these phenomena using patterns, repetition and tonality. Even nowadays, some cultures have certain instances of their music intending to imitate natural sounds. In some instances, this feature is related to shamanistic beliefs or practice. It may serve also entertainment (game) or practical (luring animals in hunt) functions.

The first instrument

It is possible that the first musical instrument was the human voice itself, which can make a vast array of sounds, from singing, humming and whistling through to clicking, coughing and yawning. The oldest known Neanderthal hyoid bone with the modern human form has been dated to be 60,000 years old, predating the oldest known bone flute by 10,000 years; but since both artifacts are unique the true chronology may date back much further! Most likely the first rhythm instruments or percussion instruments involved the clapping of hands, stones hit together, or other things that are useful to create rhythm and indeed there are examples of musical instruments which date back as far as the paleolithic (Wikipedia, 2008).

Source: José-Manuel Benito (2007). Bone flute dated in the Upper Paleolithic from Geissenklösterle, a german cave on the Swabian region. Replica. Retrieved April 30, 2013 from http://commons.wikimedia.org /wiki/File:Flauta_paleol%C3%ADtica_blanco.jpg

Now that we are ready to insert images in Moodle, let's have a look at how to capture and enhance pictures.

Capturing and enhancing pictures using GIMP

The cliché, "a picture is worth more than a thousand words", sometimes convinces me, especially if we are talking about our students creating these images by photographing, drawing, or making collages, and discussing these with their peers. Using strong images to introduce themes is a great starter and a nice context to question students. Pictures seem to resonate with many students in textbooks, course material, reports, raw material for photo stories or storyboards, and as assignment products in general. Give students a digital camera and they'll just start photographing and filming. And now it's quick and cheap to take even a thousand photos.

As teachers, we also use a lot of pictures in presentations, exams and exercises, and department or club panels, to photograph experiments and activities and students' works to create mascots made of collages and many other things. I did all of this as a teacher, and I particularly enjoyed making those mascots, for example, using the face of my school's patron with different bodies to publicize events (such as a vampire in a blood collection that was open to the community, a nurse for health week, or a mad scientist during a science week). All of these were huge successes in the school, and a great laugh too!

Let's leave the mascots aside and begin learning photo capturing.

Tips for effective photo capturing

One of the activities in our course consists of students putting together a budget for a music studio, which involves doing some research on equipment and prices, visiting real studios around their locality and taking some photos with a digital camera (a prerequisite of the course) of the solutions adopted in these studios, creating a budget using an online spreadsheet, and finally submitting everything to the course.

Giving a digital camera to students without major guidelines, especially if they are going to take photos with interior lighting in music studios, will probably result in problems of file size, lighting, and/or focus. However, let's not make it complicated—digital cameras these days can do fairly well without manual control. So let's just have a look at some basic tips for effective capturing.

There are three basic things that we should take into account while taking photos:

- Composition – how the subject (not necessarily a person) in a picture is framed
- Lighting – the sources of light and the related shadows
- Size – the number of pixels (the indivisible points) that a picture is made of

Composition

There is a basic rule of composition called the **rule of thirds** that states that the main element we want to photograph should be at one of the intersection points of four imaginary lines that divide the picture into nine equal-shaped areas.

Notice that the slider in the mixer above (the subject) is in one of these intersection points. Many digital cameras have this option to show the rule of thirds so that we can frame the picture easily by overlaying these lines in the camera's viewfinder. If not, it's just a matter of imagining the lines.

Lighting

Using a digital camera indoors can result in really bad photos. As interior lighting is usually more limited than outdoors, if we are using the camera in automatic mode, this will probably require flash or the photos will be blurry (and particularly if we are not using a tripod). Flash can be a problem if you want to keep the colors and original lighting of the interiors, and also has the limitation of giving the foreground a big burst of light while the background is left completely dark. A typical range of flash light is around one to three meters, so taking photos of a studio will almost certainly have these results.

One alternative to the flash is to use the camera with a tripod in manual mode, and control the shutter speed and aperture.

The shutter is the mechanical part that blocks all light from exposing the film (in the case of digital cameras, the CCD sensors) until you press the button. Then it quickly opens and closes, letting the light in the camera through the lens. You can control the amount of time that the shutter remains open by setting the shutter speed in your camera settings. The typical values range from $1/250^{th}$ of a second to a couple of seconds.

Aperture typically refers to the diaphragm aperture, which can be adjusted to vary the size of the pupil, and hence the amount of light that reaches the CCD sensor. Aperture is expressed in the form **f/value**, meaning that the smaller the value the larger the lens opening (aperture). There is a so-called Sunny 16 rule that states that an approximately correct exposure will be obtained on a sunny day by using an aperture of f/16 and a shutter speed close to the reciprocal of the ISO speed of the film; for example, using ISO 200 film, an aperture of f/16, and a shutter speed of 1/200 second.

In a place with little light, for example, we could use a low value for the f/value (f/2.8) and a higher value for the shutter speed (for example, 1/3). With these settings, we won't be able to hold our camera steady for 1/3 second, so the secret is to use a tripod, and if necessary, a delayed shutter so that our fingers don't shake the camera while taking the photo.

Here's a photo of a studio wall covered with egg boxes, taken with these settings and a tripod:

This kept the actual room lighting pretty much the same and the picture focused (except on the right, where the tips of the egg boxes were too close to the lens).

Size

When we buy a digital camera, we usually look at the maximum number of megapixels (millions of pixels, the elementary points of which a photo is comprised) of the photos it can take, but we should look at other things as well, such as the quality of the lens. "The bigger the better" is not always true, and in the case of digital photos, if we just want to make small prints or use them on our computer and on the Web, a size of 2 megapixels (1600 x 1200 pixels) is more than enough! If the main goal is this, taking photos with 7 megapixels will be just silly; we'll need more space (this means more expensive camera cards to store photos and bigger computer hard disks), and more time to transfer the photos to our computer. Even 1,600 x 1,200 pixels is too much if we want, for example, to post one of these pictures in a forum post in Moodle; it would result in horizontal or vertical scrolling, as the photo would be too big for a typical screen size. The best solution is to resize them to a proper width using an image editing software. Note that nowadays, it's hard to get just a 2 megapixels camera, but if we were to buy a 7 megapixels camera, we could change the settings to take photos with just 2 megapixels.

Enhancing pictures using GIMP

With photos, digital drawings, or pictures taken from the Web, we will need to crop, resize, rotate, correct, or compose them, so this will be the time to look at these common procedures. And we will do this with a free image editing software application called **GIMP**.

GIMP (http://www.gimp.org) is a cross-platform free software application for creating and modifying images and a nice alternative to commercial software such as Adobe Photoshop. With this tool, we can do various tasks, right from simple resize and crop operations to complex character drawing and photo editing. There are simple tools included in the Microsoft Windows as well, such as Paint or Windows Photo Viewer, that allow resizing and cropping. However, starting with GIMP to do these operations will get us used to the interface from the beginning of our course, so that later on we can do more complex operations such as photo editing.

 At the time of writing this book, GIMP 2.8.4 is the latest release and hence all of the procedures used in this chapter refer to this release. The latest release may differ in terms of the GUI and may have some additional functionality.

After we download GIMP from `http://gimp.org/downloads` and install it, we will notice something different about this software as soon as we open it.

There isn't a single window that contains several smaller windows, so if you are feeling a little bit confused, don't worry. After using it for some time, we will get used to it really quickly!

The GIMP standard interface has some main elements as seen in the following screenshot:

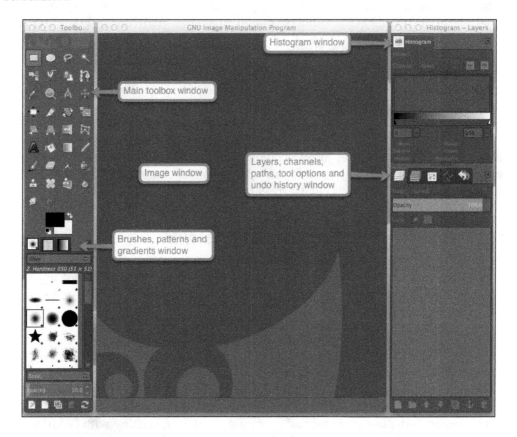

- **The main toolbox window**: This window is the heart of GIMP. It contains the highest-level menu and a set of icon buttons that can be used to select tools, and more. If you close it, GIMP closes.

- **The image window**: Each image opened in GIMP is displayed in a separate window. Many images can be open at the same time; the limit is set only by the amount of system resources.

- **The brushes, patterns, and gradients window**: Docked below the main toolbox is a window showing options for brushes, patterns, and gradients.

- **The histogram window**: This window shows a histogram for the picture being edited.

- **The layers, channels, paths, tool options, and undo history window**: This window shows the layer structure of the currently active image, and allows it to be manipulated in a variety of ways. It is possible to do a few very basic things without using the layers dialog, but even moderately sophisticated GIMP users will find it indispensable to have the layers dialog available at all times. There are tabs for other settings, as for example the tool options, showing options for the currently selected tool.

Restoring GIMP's standard interface

Sometimes, by accident, we might close one of these elements. If this happens, select the Windows menu item **Recently closed docks**, wherein we can finally select the dock we closed.

Cropping

In several modules of the course *Music for everyday life*, we will need to resize photos and screenshots so that they can be easily displayed in a web browser in typical screen sizes, usually 1,024 x 768 or even 1,280 x 1,024 pixels. Let's work on an image from *Tears of Steel*, an open short movie for which our students will have to create a movie trailer and add a soundtrack in *Module 3, Music and media*.

This image will give the context to this activity and we will add it to the task description in the activity **Soundtrackers**. There is a problem though—the images available on the website of the movie, for example `http://mango.blender.org/gallery/`, are too large to fit a standard Moodle course page. If we added the image as is, we would get something similar to the following:

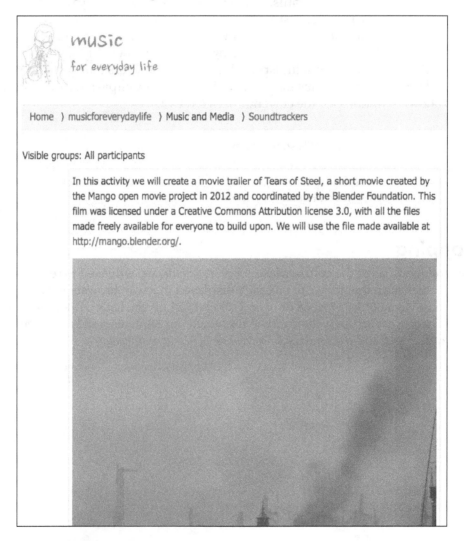

The problem of using an image of this size in Moodle is obvious, so we will solve it by first cropping the image and then resizing it. We will crop the image because there's additional information in it that is not necessary for what we want, which is just to give some context to the activity. We will then resize it because it will be still too large to fit the course aptly.

So let's first open the original image in GIMP after downloading it to our computer. For this we should perform the following steps:

1. Go to the **File** menu and click on **Open...**.
2. Select the picture that we saved to our computer, and click on **Open**.

After the picture is opened in the image window, we will start by selecting the region of the picture that we want to crop using, of course, the Crop tool in the **Toolbox** pane.

Don't forget that we can use the mouse to identify the functions of the buttons just by waiting a second with the mouse pointer over them. We are then ready to drag around the area we want. So, basically, for cropping perform the following steps:

1. Select the Crop tool in the **Toolbox** pane.
2. In the image window, left-click on the upper-left corner and with the mouse button held down, drag the mouse to the bottom-right corner to the desired size (for example, 1024 x 768). Don't worry if you are not being precise.
3. Double-click at the middle of the selected picture area.

Note that there will be a shaded part of the picture and this area will be cropped. Also, note the squares at the corners of the selection. We can use these to adjust the crop area. When we double-click at the center of the selected area, we will obtain a picture similar to the following:

Resizing

The picture we cropped is still too large for our course (around 1200 pixels wide). As a result, before we insert it in our **Soundtrackers** activity, we will need to resize it. The HTML editor allows resizing of the photo, but the problem is that the image loses quality. The best thing to do is resize it in GIMP. Now the obvious question would be, "What works as a good size for Moodle courses?" As a reference for the width of pictures in Moodle, we can use the following values (considering a typical screen size of 1024 x 768 and a standard theme):

Picture width	When to use
480 px	If the image is used inside a topic (as a topic title or label)
160 px	If the image is used inside a side block
640 to 800 px	If the image is used inside a Moodle resource or activity (for example, a forum post)

Resizing this image width to 640 px will make it look good in our course activity.

The procedure to resize it is as follows:

1. From the top menu, click on **Image** and then **Scale Image...**.

2. Define a new **Width:** value in the form (**640** pixels in this case). Notice the chain icon on the right. If you click on it, the width and height will not be relative, so you can deform the picture.

3. Click on the **Scale** button.

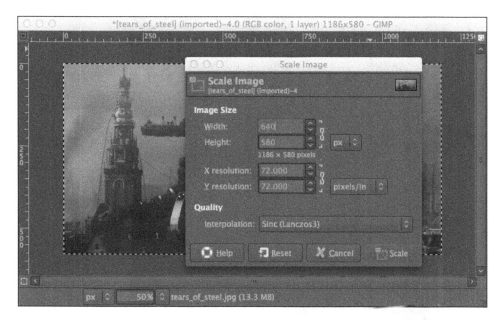

And the resize is done. Now, we just need to save it and upload it on our Moodle activity.

Saving (exporting)

The original picture format of JPEG can be used in Moodle without great problems, so we will just need to save the cropped-then-resized version of our original. To do this, we should go to the **File** menu, and click on **Export...**.

We can select the desired picture format using either of two methods in GIMP. The first is really simple—in the **Name:** field form at the top of the window, we just need to type the intended extension. GIMP will recognize this and convert the image to the desired format. In our case, we will keep the JPEG format, so we will name the file image_name.jpg. GIMP will then recognize that we want to save the image in the JPEG format.

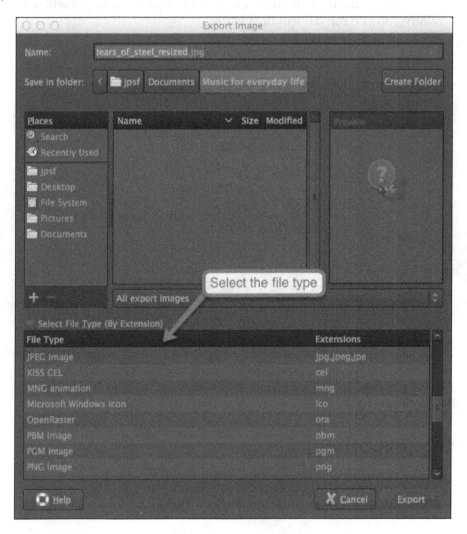

The second way to select the desired image format is through the interface. To do this, perform the following steps:

1. Go to the bottom of the **Export Image** window and click on the arrow button next to the text **Select File Type (By Extension)**.
2. Select the desired image format.
3. Select the destination folder in **Places**.
4. Click on the **Export** button.

And finally, after inserting the image in our Moodle activity **Soundtrackers** (using the HTML editor as we saw previously), we will get something similar to the following screenshot:

Rotating

Sometimes when we photograph a scene with a straight line in the background (the horizon is the best example but in a music studio the same can happen), if we are not using a tripod, it's easy to get skewed photos. We can correct these mistakes in GIMP by using the **Rotate** tool, which is the button to the right of the Crop button in **Toolbox**.

To rotate an image, we can do the following after opening the image file:

1. Select the Rotate tool from **Toolbox**.

2. Click on the image.

3. A pop-up window will appear. We can use the slider to adjust the image or enter a value for the **Angle:** field (negative values if you want to rotate the image counterclockwise).

4. Click on the **Rotate** button.

5. In the end, we can use the Crop tool to eliminate areas of the photo that are missing.

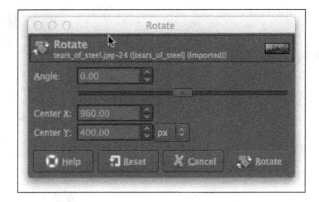

Flipping and rotating

Flipping and rotating are very easy tasks to perform in GIMP. If we need to flip an image horizontally or vertically, or rotate it (for example, 90° clockwise), we just need to go to the **Layer** menu, click on **Transform**, and select the required option from the submenu.

Correcting white balance and color

In situations with bad lighting, for example, incandescent light, we will need to correct the white balance, and in worse situations, the color balance of the photo.

We can do this in the following three ways:

- Using the auto white balance function
- Adjusting the levels
- Adjusting the color balance

One quick alternative is to use the auto white balance function of GIMP. Go to **Colors | Auto | White Balance**.

If the auto white balance doesn't do the trick, the second option is to use the **Levels** tool. Go to **Colors | Levels...**. You can then use the Eye Dropper tool on the left in the Levels window to choose a point in the photo that is completely black and the one on the right for a completely white point. If you can't get both points, try to get one and check the results.

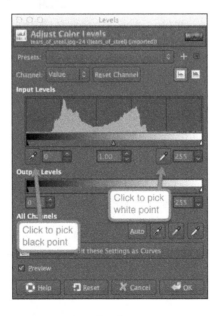

The third option is to use the color balance function. Go to **Colors | Color Balance...**. We can adjust the color levels and compensate for any lack or excess of a particular color, by selecting the range of colors (**Shadows**, **Midtones**, or **Highlights**) and using the slides for each of the color levels.

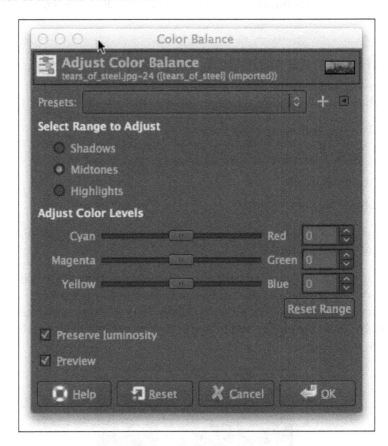

Correcting brightness and contrast

If the photos are over exposed (there is extra light), we can reduce the brightness and compensate with the contrast to improve the quality. Go to **Colors | Brightness-Contrast...**. This can also be used to intensify the contrast of the photo, giving it well-defined shadows. However, note that when we use all of these options, the photo loses information, and if we are not careful, the resulting image can be worse than the original one.

We have now seen how to capture and enhance photos and images in general. Let's now see other useful actions that we can perform on pictures.

Let's see how we can make photo collages, a way of combining several images to make a new one, again using GIMP.

Creating digital photo collages

Photo collages are a great way to make posters, site headers, CD art, flyers, certificates, or storyboards. They basically consist of placing together parts from several pictures to make a new one. This can be done on paper of course, and then scanned or photographed to convert it to a digital format (try it, it's fun), or we can do the whole process digitally using GIMP.

In our course, in *Module 7, Music and the commons*, students are required to edit a CD made of music selections or their own music. In this CD, they will need to create a CD cover. This will be a good context to introduce the photo collage technique.

As we are combining different photos into a single one, we should create a folder to keep all the photos and a project file. GIMP, besides saving in JPEG, PNG, and many other formats, also has one dedicated format for projects that contain several layers called **XCF**. So as an example, I have created the cd_cover.xcf file and a folder called photos as shown in the following screenshot:

An important concept in photo collages is layers. Let's start with this concept.

Adding layers

Layers can be compared in some ways to audio and video projects as kind of tracks, where we can insert pictures and combine them in a final project.

The first thing to do in our photo collage is to get a nice background image, and at least one other image to work as a layer to add on top of the background. The procedure for adding layers is as follows:

1. Open the picture that we want to use as a background for the montage by going to **File | Open** or by pressing *Ctrl + O* (*command + O* for Mac users).

2. Make sure that the **Layers** dialog box is visible. If it is not, we can select **Windows | Dockable Dialogs | Layers** or use the *Ctrl + L* shortcut.

3. In the **Layers** tab, double-click on the text next to the thumbnail of the image and change it to Background.

4. Open the picture that we want to combine with the first one (go to **File | Open** or press *Ctrl + O*). This will open a new window.

5. In this new window, select the picture (go to **Select | All** or press *Ctrl + A*).

6. Copy it to the clipboard by going to **Edit | Copy** or by pressing *Ctrl + C*.

7. Click on the background image window.

8. Paste the picture by going to **Edit | Paste** or by pressing *Ctrl + V*.

GIMP will automatically create a new layer called **Floating Selection (Pasted Layer),** which can be seen in the **Layers** dialog box.

We have to make sure that the photo we have pasted is smaller than the one in the background. Cropping or resizing it before this can be useful. However, it doesn't need to have the final size for publishing, as we will be able to resize it later as a layer.

In the **Layers** dialog box, we can also change the name of the layers in our project by double-clicking on one of the layers, which can be helpful if we have many.

Eliminating photo areas

It's a common procedure in photo collages to eliminate some of the photo's areas such as backgrounds, or cutting around the profile of a person to isolate them. We will use a technique called **Layer Mask** that will help us do this easily. To do this, first open the **Layers** dialog box and follow these steps:

1. Double-click on the text **Floating Selection (Pasted Layer)** in the **Layers** window and change the name of the layer (for example, Foreground). Right-click and select the **Add Layer Mask** option.

2. We are given some options, and the default one is what we need: **White (full opacity)**. So let's click on **Add**.

We get something similar to the following screenshot in the **Layers** dialog box:

Note that we can click either on the thumbnail of the picture or on the thumbnail of the mask (in white, to the right of the thumbnail). We should click on the latter to start removing the background.

To remove the background, we need to select the Paintbrush tool in **Toolbox**, with black as the foreground. When we start painting our foreground image in the selected areas, these will become transparent. To correct any mistakes, we should invert the foreground and background colors and paint with the brush in white, and the original image will return again. Control the zoom and the brush scale to get more or less detail.

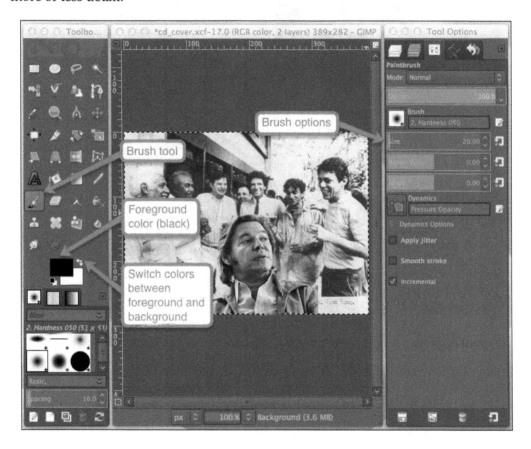

Once we are done, we can scale this layer by going to **Layer** | **Scale Layer** (don't go to **Image** | **Scale**, as this will cause the entire image, including all layers, to be resized) and place it where we want it by using the Move tool.

Adding text

Finally, let's add some text to it. Using the Text tool, we can enter some text in the GIMP text editor. A new layer will be created for this.

In the tool options, we can select the font, size, and other attributes for the text.

We can now save the file in the XCF format to keep all of the layer's information (**File | Save as...**). After that, we can export it (**File | Export...**) to a more usable format for the Web, such as PNG, and publish it on Moodle, for example, as a forum attachment with ratings. Several CD covers proposed by students can be voted and the winner selected.

Capturing screenshots

Capturing screenshots can be very useful if we are doing the following:

- Creating a how to document on using a computer application and the need to illustrate the procedures

- Creating a presentation about some online resources and showing how they look (assuming that we don't have an Internet connection during the presentation)

- Getting some frames from a video (for example, a DVD or a Web-based video)

- Keeping records of webshots (website screenshots) that we find interesting, in order to post on our blog or in Moodle (for example, a portfolio of some websites that we have developed)

We can take screenshots in one of the following ways:

- Using the *Print Screen* function supported by the majority of computers (and keyboards) to capture the entire screen or a specific application window

- Using GIMP

- Using Jing (`http://www.techsmith.com/jing.html`) to directly capture a region of the screen (and insert callouts on it, such as the screenshots used in this book)

The first technique is fairly easy, we just have to hit the *Print Screen* key, or in a Mac, *command + shift + 3*, and save the file in our Desktop. So, let's start with the second technique, that is, using GIMP.

Capturing screenshots using GIMP

In the final course module, to wrap up we will require students to create a digital portfolio of their best works from the course. This will involve capturing screenshots of some of the products of the course and later creating a narrated video where they have to comment on these screenshots (we will see how to create these narrated videos in *Chapter 5, Understanding Web-based Applications and Other Multimedia Forms*). For now, we will look at an example of a screenshot of an online map that students have to build in *Module 1, Music evolves*, showing the location of some instruments on a world map and some of its characteristics.

The steps for a screen capture are as follows:

1. Prepare the window on the desktop that we want to capture. In this case, it will be a browser window opened on our map.

2. Open GIMP, go to **File | Create | Screenshot**, and select the option **Take a screenshot of a single window**.

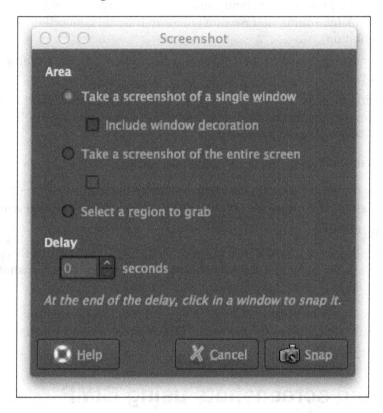

An image window will open, containing the captured screenshot that we can now edit and save. We should then export it to save it in a proper image format to use in Moodle.

The captured screenshot will look similar to the following screenshot:

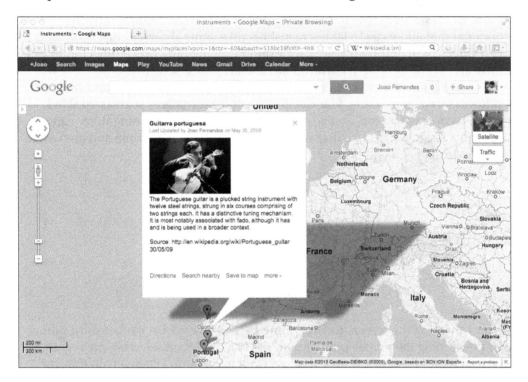

In both cases, there are some issues that we should consider before taking a screenshot. One of the first things we need to bear in mind is that if we want to use the screenshot in a web page or document, it should have an appropriate size. For this, we should reduce the window sizes and elements that we want to capture and fit them to standard sizes adequate to our medium, minimizing all of the empty space and increasing the letter size if necessary. To have a look at copyright issues concerning screenshots, refer to *Chapter 8, Common Multimedia Issues in Moodle*.

Capturing screenshots using Jing

Jing (`http://www.techsmith.com/jing.html`) is a screen capture software application that allows us to take screenshots (like some shown in this book) and screen videos (with our own voice), for example, explaining procedures for a piece of software. These desktop recordings are usually called screencasts (and we will see how to make them in *Chapter 4, Video*) and can be made in both Mac and Microsoft Windows (sorry Linux users, you can find several alternatives such as vnc2swf, xvidcap, recordmydesktop, and so on). After installing and running it, we can access it through a "sunny" interface that we can access and move anytime and anywhere on the desktop.

To start capturing the screen, the first thing to do is to click on the left-most button (after positioning the mouse pointer over the sun) and then selecting the region of the screen or application window that we want to capture. When we do this, the frame around the area to capture has a small menu on its bottom-left corner (refer to the following screenshot) with the options Image, Video, Redo selection, and Cancel.

Clicking on the Image button reveals some of the advantages of Jing over the previous technique. The first one is that it allows us to comment directly on the captured image, giving us a set of tools to do it.

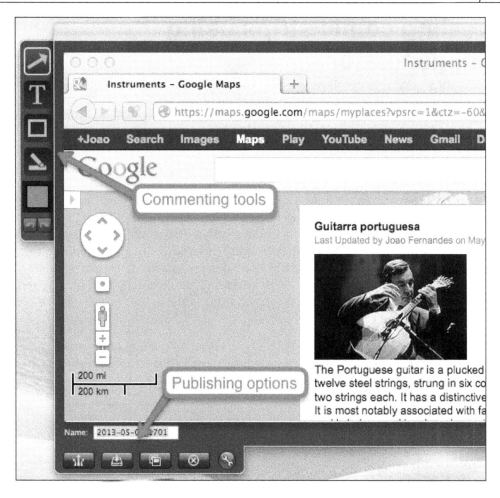

To cancel a capture, we just need to press the right mouse button or select something and then click on the Cancel button. Once we have selected an area to capture, we can save it by clicking on the Save button (the second from the left) in the publishing options below the captured area. Note that we can publish the screenshots directly to our Flickr account (for example) by adding a customized button (click on the last button in the publishing options and explore).

One of Jing's limitations is that if we take a capture, comment it, and save it; we cannot correct or change what we did in the exported file. So we will have to create a new commented screenshot.

Creating comic strips using Stripgenerator

Comics are a great way of telling a story. They can be used to do the following:

- Creating hypothetical situations that could happen in real life (for example, a conflict or a funny situation)
- Creating a storyboard for a movie
- Narrating an event

If you are getting worried that we will have to draw something and your skills are, well, those of a 10-year old kid, that's not a problem as mine aren't that good either! Fortunately, there's a tool just for you and me called **Stripgenerator**, which will save us from further humiliation in front of our students and colleagues. In our course in Moodle, in *Module 5*, *Being a musician*, we will design an activity where students have to create a story based on a day in the life of a musician, and they will be required to use this tool to illustrate this. We can then add this work to the Moodle course easily as an attachment to a forum.

Stripgenerator (`http://stripgenerator.com/`) is an online tool for creating comic strips with an easy-to-use drag-and-drop interface that makes creating comics look simple.

You can see some of the examples that other comic strip artists did by going to the strip blog gallery or by searching for some keywords. Here's one as an example about a lesson in sharing:

Source: fanton (2007, April 26). A lesson in sharing. Retrieved October 17, 2009, from http://welcometocartoon.
stripgenerator.com/2007/04/26/a-lesson-in-sharing.html

Adding elements

To start a comic strip, you'll first have to create an account. Once you are done with that, click on the **CREATE NEW STRIP** button on the right.

We are then presented with the following workspace to start building the comic strip:

On the top of the blank strip, we can see some tabs. This is where we can select frames, characters, items, text, check the library, or get theme packs. The three white rectangles (frames) are actually where we will make our story by dragging the elements from the top into them. Note that we can't upload any pictures, so we are limited to the elements provided.

The editing tools in the toolbar below the three frames allow us to delete elements, send them to the back of other elements, flip, format text in bubbles, zoom in or out, and so on. We just need to hover the mouse over these buttons to see their functions.

When we add an element to a frame, we can also move, resize, or rotate it, by either dragging it around or by using the small boxes on the object's boundary.

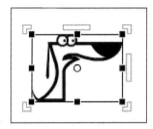

Publishing

After we are done creating a comic strip, we just have to follow these steps to publish it to Moodle:

1. Click on **Finish**. If we don't do this and navigate away from the page, we might lose all of our work.

2. Give a title and a description to the strip, add some tags, and click on the **Publish** button.

After we publish it, we see the final result, and if we click on the tab **Share&Promote**, we get information for embedding the strip on our course or a direct image link if we want to save the image to our computer and then upload it to Moodle as a forum attachment, as seen in the following screenshot:

Now that we know how to create comic strips, let's have a look at some basic procedures that we can execute to integrate presentations into our courses.

Creating slideshows

Slideshows are a great way of presenting information and supporting discussions; so, we will have a look at the following things that can be useful in Moodle courses:

- Converting presentation slides to images in order to integrate them in a Moodle lesson
- Sharing our presentations through an online service and then embedding them in Moodle
- Creating photo slideshows on the Web to later embed them in a Moodle resource or activity

Exporting PowerPoint slides as images to build Moodle lessons

An easy way to create an exercise in our Moodle courses is to build a lesson around a presentation that we used in class, for example, in Microsoft PowerPoint. This will provide the content and then we can add some questions, working with the existing material and not having to rebuild it again in the Moodle lesson. The easiest way to do this is to convert the PowerPoint (or similar) presentation to images and then add these images to branch tables or question pages in our lesson.

The problem with this is that the image width of standard slides will be 960 pixels, a little bit large as we saw for a Moodle course. To overcome this problem (without having to resize each image in GIMP), after opening the presentation we should change the slide width and height before exporting them as images. We can do this by going to the **Themes** tab, clicking on the **Slide size options** button, and then clicking on the **Page Setup** option, as shown in the following screenshot:

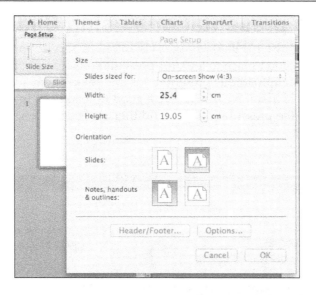

By setting both width and height values to half of their current values (in cm, check the following conversion to get the equivalent pixels), we will get images with a width of 480 pixels, which is a good size for inserting them in a lesson. If this size makes the text in the slides look too small, we can use a width of 640 pixels. So, we would use the following values:

Desired width (pixels)	Width (cm)	Height (cm)
480	9,52	12,7
640	12,7	16,93

So now we are ready to export our presentation, by opening the presentation and then going to **File** | **Save as Pictures** (the default image format is JPEG) and saving it to a folder. Each slide will be a separate image. We can then add it to a Moodle lesson, for example, just like adding a regular picture in Moodle.

One drawback of this technique is accessibility, as the text in the images will not be read by screen readers. A possible solution for this is to add a good description text to the images while inserting them using the HTML editor in Moodle.

Publishing presentations using SlideShare

SlideShare (http://www.slideshare.net) is an online service for sharing presentations. It is a good place to look for presentations for our courses. It's also a place where we can upload our presentations and make them available to many. Another advantage is that if we don't have a good upload limit in our Moodle course; we can add the presentation here and then embed it in our course!

To publish a presentation in SlideShare, we just need to create an account and upload our presentation in several supported formats (Microsoft PowerPoint or Apache Open Office Impress, PDF, and so on). SlideShare will generate code necessary to put our presentation anywhere on the Web.

So, after signing in, let's upload the presentation by clicking on the **Upload** link at the top of the screen and then filling in the required forms.

When we click on the **UPLOAD** button, we need to navigate to the destination and select the file that we want to upload. We should then fill in the details with some information about the presentation and allow (or not) readers to download our presentation.

After we click on the **Save changes** button, we can then get the embed code required to add it to our Moodle course.

In *Module 7, Music and the commons*, a presentation made available through this service is used.

Creating online photo slideshows using Animoto

Animoto (`http://animoto.com`) is a web application that allows us to create photo slideshows either using the images uploaded from our computer or from images that are already on the Web (in services such as Flickr). And we don't need to install any software!

This can be helpful in our course *Module 5, Being a musician,* where students have to create a photo story of their favorite artist.

After signing up, we should hit the **CREATE** button in the front page and then select one of the free available styles. These styles allow us to create short 30-second photo slideshows with a predefined template for free.

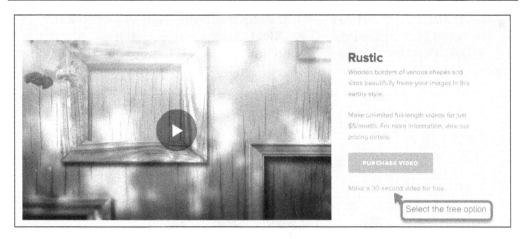

We are then taken to the slideshow production page, where we can add pictures (from our computer or from services such as Flickr and Instagram), change the soundtrack, or add titles and captions.

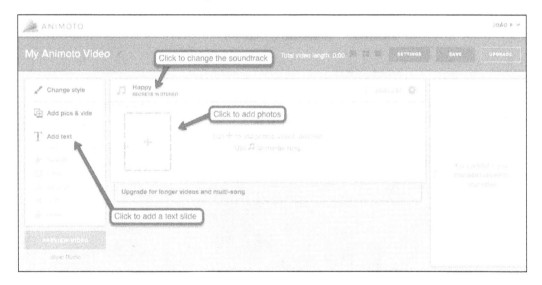

We can drag-and-drop pictures and text slides to reorder them and when we are set, we should click on the **PREVIEW VIDEO** button. Notice that if we upload more images than the allowed 30-second limit, these will show on the right of the sequencer in the so called tray.

A low resolution preview of the photo slideshow is then presented, and we can fill in some details and produce it, that is, publish it.

The final video will show up, and to get the embed code, we should click on the
More button:

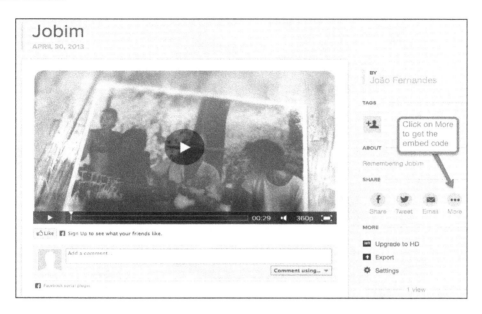

Finally, we just have to copy the embed code displayed in the tab **Embedded video**.

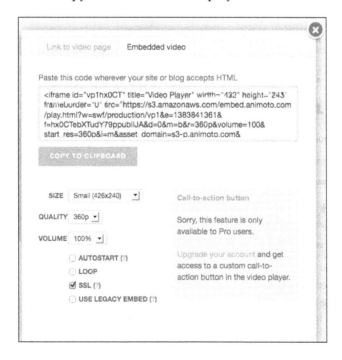

And at last, paste it to Moodle (remembering to use the HTML edit mode), and we get something like this:

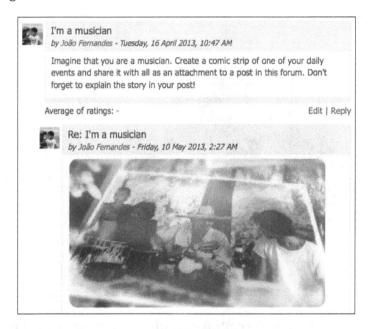

Summary

In this chapter, we started by seeing how to find free pictures online to add to our course materials (and assignments, from a student's perspective) in services such as Flickr and Wikimedia Commons. We then had a look at different ways of inserting images in Moodle, especially using the HTML editor's image upload function. We then started using GIMP for main image editing tasks, such as cropping, resizing, capturing (together with some photography concepts), color correction, photo collage, and saving the images in different formats. Some issues regarding images in Moodle, such as file formats and appropriate sizes, were also discussed and we used GIMP and Jing to collect screenshots. Stripgenerator was also used to easily create comic strips. We also learned how to export PowerPoint presentations to images, adding them to a Moodle lesson, or as an alternative to publishing these presentations in SlideShare. We concluded this chapter by looking at ways to create photo slideshows using Animoto.

Now it's time to put your headphones on! Audio is our next job. We will learn how to find free music and sounds online, understand basic audio formats and settings, use free software for audio editing, extract audio from CDs, create voice recordings, and integrate them in Moodle.

3
Sound and Music

This chapter focuses on creating and editing sound and music for the course *Music for everyday life*. This involves finding free audio online, creating our own voice recordings, remixing audio, podcasting, and even converting text to speech.

By the end of this chapter you will be able to do the following:

- Finding free music and sounds online for your multimedia projects
- Selecting appropriate audio formats and settings according to your needs
- Using a set of free software tools for common procedures in sound and music editing
- Extracting audio from CDs
- Creating voice recordings
- Integrating all of these into Moodle

Finding free music and sounds online

As with pictures, the usual suspect for finding free audio tracks online is again Wikimedia Commons. This is a huge database of multimedia elements, and we can find interesting stuff there. But before we look into these, let's start with the basics of audio formats so that we can pick better files for our courses.

The basics of audio formats

In our everyday life, we can find music and sound in several formats. The most common of these formats are:

- **PCM**: This is the standard format used in CDs. It is an uncompressed audio format, which implies large file sizes—around 10 MB per minute.

- **WAV**: WAV is usually used to store the PCM file format. It can contain audio in several rates and bitrates (these are concepts that we will see in a moment).

- **MP3**: MPEG Layer 3 is one of the most common audio formats on the Web. It is also the name of the codec that reduces original audio files sizes (for example, depending on the bitrate and rate, a CD track can be reduced to 1/10th the size of the original file size).

- **WMA**: Windows Media Audio is the standard audio format released by Microsoft.

- **OGG**: OCG is an open source file format that can contain several codecs, Vorbis being the most common.

- **MIDI**: The MIDI format is an industry standard for electronic music, allowing electronic musical instruments, computer software, and other equipments to communicate. For example, a MIDI keyboard uses MIDI to communicate with a computer. You have probably heard a MIDI file before, usually a very small sized file, which sounds like electronic music from the 80s (yes, they were used quite a lot in those weird times). However, as MIDI files don't actually have audio waveforms in them, it is possible to associate real instrument sounds to MIDI instructions and have nice sounding files.

There are four concepts to keep in mind while dealing with audio files (and video files, as we will see in the next chapter), namely **file format**, **codec**, **rate**, and **bitrate**.

The file format is the easy one—whatever extension a file has, that is its file format, for example, MP3, WAV, and OGG. The codec does the processing of the data inside the file; so for example, in OGG, it can use the Vorbis audio codec.

In addition to these two, rate and bitrate refer to the number of times per second that an original audio is sampled and stored in Hz, the same as 1/second, and the number of bits that are processed in every unit of time (Kb/s) respectively.

I would recommend MP3 as a working format for our daily needs (in Moodle or anywhere else), in which we can use different rates and bitrates according to our goal; for example, make a song excerpt from a CD available or add voice to forums. Check the following table for some reference values that will be useful later on:

Rate	Bitrate	When to use
44,100 Hz	128 Kb/s	To rip CDs and use in most cases
11,025 Hz	48 Kb/s	To record voice for a daily use (interviews, students answers, comments, and so on)

Now that we know this, let's start by finding free sound tracks and free music on the Web for our audio projects.

Internet Archive – audio archive

The Internet Archive (`http://www.archive.org`) is an online library that provides permanent access to historical material on the Web, a kind of "memory" of the Web. We can see this in action, for example, in the Wayback Machine (`http://www.archive.org/web/web.php`), where we have access to static versions of web pages from their start to the present day, with some of the archiving starting as far as 1996 (this can be a really fun activity!). One of the subprojects of this initiative is the Audio Archive (`http://www.archive.org/details/audio`), a library with over one million free digital recordings, ranging from old radio shows to concerts and poetry readings.

We can either search this collection using the search form or explore the subcollections.

Freesound

Freesound (http://www.freesound.org) is a collaborative collection of sounds licensed under a Creative Commons license, allowing us to use them in our own works.

CCMixter

CCMixter (http://ccmixter.org) is a project from the Creative Commons initiative, where we can find lots of samples to use in our audio projects. We can also upload the results to the same site. All of the content is licensed under Creative Commons licenses.

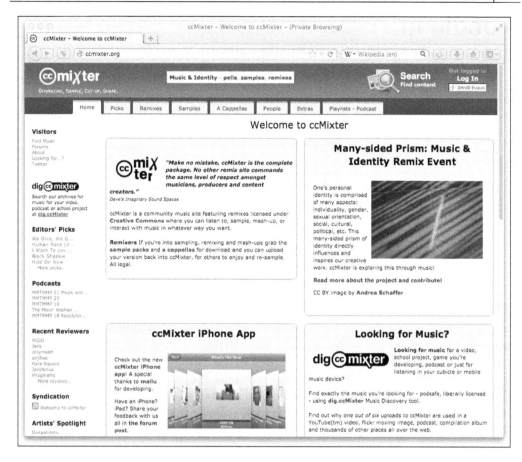

Other music and sound sites

In addition to the services that we saw earlier, we can also find music and sounds for free at the following links:

- Musopen (http://www.musopen.com) – an online music library of public domain music
- Soundbible (http://soundbible.com) – an online library of free sound effects and sound clips

Before we get into the details of how to create audio for our course, let's have a quick look at how we can integrate audio into Moodle. We could start by downloading an audio file from the WIRED CD http://creativecommons.org/wired and then Moodle it!

Moodle it!

To integrate audio into Moodle, we have two options:

- Upload an audio file in the course and then link to it by using any text editor. If Moodle has the multimedia filter working, and if we are talking about MP3 files, a flash player will automatically be inserted to play the file. We have seen this in *Chapter 1, Getting Ready for Multimedia in Moodle*.

The flash player in Moodle only accepts MP3 files with a sample rate of 11.025, 22.050, or 44.100 kHz, a bitrate below 128 Kbps, and preferably CBR (Constant Bit Rate) over VBR (Variable Bit Rate). Usually, you won't have problems, but if you hear a chipmunk-like sound when you play one of these files in Moodle, the problem will probably be in one of these properties.

- Upload an audio file to an online service and then embed it in Moodle.

The same applies to other audio formats recognized by the multimedia plugin in Moodle (in audio, Real Player for now, in video others such as Windows Media Player or Apple QuickTime). In this case, we will need to have the players installed in our computer and these will be embedded in the Moodle course. However, the easiest one is MP3, as we just need the flash plugin. We can convert any audio to MP3 using **Audacity**, a tool we will explore in a moment. So now that we have the sources for our raw materials, let's have a look at how we can build on the work of others and create our own audio.

Creating and delivering

In school, as a teacher, most of the work that I did in audio with students had to do with soundtracks for small movies, combining, for example, voice and music for a documentary about a nature reserve (the Sado river, near Lisbon, a beautiful place). They voted for the best voice, after some auditions and recordings, and picked some of the songs for the soundtrack, later combining them into groups by using Windows Movie Maker as a draft. Later on, their work was used in Adobe Premiere and Encore to produce a DVD. These are some examples of what we can do with audio, but there are many others, such as:

- Radios (online or regular) and all sorts of programs
- Interviews
- Critiques or commentaries of CDs, songs, movies, books, or articles

- Music CDs and podcasts
- Audio books
- Video soundtracks
- Discussions in Moodle forums with voice or instruments' recordings

Let's start off with a simple task, that is, finding and managing audio using Grooveshark.

Finding and managing audio using Grooveshark

Grooveshark (`http://www.grooveshark.com`) is a community for music sharing where we can find and upload music, broadcast our own radio, create playlists, and embed them in Moodle (and other websites).

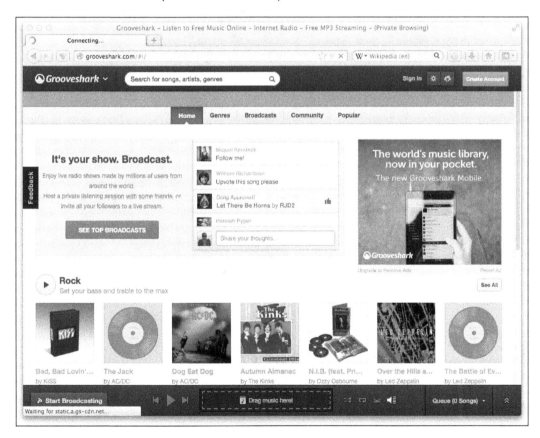

We can now have a look at how to upload audio and create playlists in Grooveshark, something that can be used easily in our course in order to give it some musicality! And this doesn't mean that we can only use this for music-related courses. Every course is a good course to have music on!

Uploading audio to Grooveshark

Uploading in Grooveshark is easy. Again with the WIRED CD `http://creativecommons.org/wired` as a source of music files, we just need to follow these steps:

1. Click on the **Upload** button in the top bar.

2. Accept the terms and allow the Java plugin to run.

3. Select the file from our computer, click on the **Continue** button, and fill in some details (title, artist, album, year, and so on).

The uploaded files will be listed on our **Collection** list, reachable through the top menu.

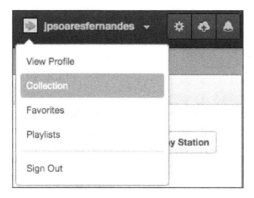

In this collection we can manage our uploaded audio.

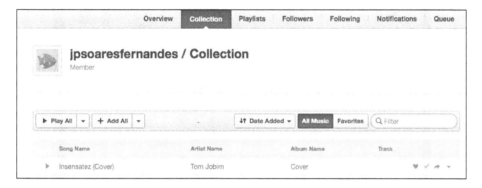

Creating playlists in Grooveshark

Instead of having just one song embedded in our Moodle course, we can have an entire sequence of songs, called a **playlist**. To create a playlist from our uploads (or from the list of songs made available by other users), in the right frame, we should click on **Create** Playlist and add a title and description to our new playlist. And then, it's as easy as searching for songs and dragging it from the results to the playlist.

After the playlist has all of the songs that you want, you can click on the **Playlist** name and organize it (for example, changing the order of the songs with drag-and-drop and deleting songs).

Moodle it!

Now to get the embed code to add the playlist to Moodle, we must click on the **Share** button and then on the **Embed** tab, copying the code.

In our course, a playlist was added in every module's delivery moment to have students experience different music styles and artists.

A playlist was also added to a side block on the main course page as a kind of "course soundtrack".

To embed a particular song, if we hover the mouse over its name, a kind of hyperlink shows up. If we click on it, we are taken to the song page and there we can get the embed code, just like for the playlists.

Extracting audio from CDs using VLC

While teaching several subjects, particularly related to music and language, audio can be extremely useful, almost mandatory. We can give students the opportunity to listen to interviews, stories, audio books, dialogs, music, or even their own voices. More than that, we can give them the opportunity to create all of these on their own.

One of our course modules will be dedicated to *Module 3*, *Music and media*, and one of the main tasks in this module, the Soundtrackers activity will be to create a soundtrack for a movie trailer of Tears of Steel (something we saw in the *Chapter 2*, *Picture This*, while cropping and resizing pictures). Students will make this soundtrack from songs and sound effects. Let's first focus on the music, and see how we can extract audio from The WIRED CD (`http://creativecommons.org/wired`) as an example:

Note that we are using a CD that is not copyright protected for this task. These instructions will still work with most copyright protected CDs (which include most CDs that you buy), but be careful that you are not breaking any laws by doing so. Please have a look at *Chapter 8*, *Common Multimedia Issues in Moodle*, for some advice on this.

VLC Media Player (`http://www.videolan.org/vlc`) is a free, cross-platform media player that can play almost any available media file. This can be very important for video, as there is an incredible variety of video codecs that are available these days (DivX, Xvid, H.264, and so on), encapsulated in many container formats (AVI, MP4, ASF, WMV, MOV, and so on). But before we get to work with video, let's start with something simpler, that is, audio.

VLC can be used to play and extract audio from a CD. Audio CDs have been available since 1982 and are used to store music by using a technique called **PCM encoding**. However, we will use the MP3 format in our Moodle course for several reasons:

- The files have smaller sizes
- Moodle has a MP3 filter that automatically puts a player in place so that we can listen to the song without downloading it, simply by clicking on the play button
- MP3-format songs are easy to edit and to create podcasts from because MP3 has become the standard for sound and music files

We will first convert some of the tracks of this audio CD to MP3 files on our hard disks. This is what we call ripping. So first, let's put the WIRED CD in the CD player of our computer and choose the tracks for our soundtrack.

 At the time of writing this book, VLC Media Player 2.0.6 is the latest release, and hence all of the procedures used in this chapter refer to this release. The latest release may differ in terms of the GUI and may have some additional functionality.

Ripping a CD track

VLC has a wizard that is helpful in defining the settings to rip the CD track to an MP3 format.

1. Open the VLC media player and go to **File | Streaming/Exporting Wizard...**.

2. Select the **Transcode/Save to file** option.

3. Click on the **Next** button as shown in the following screenshot:

In the next window, we need to select a stream (the source that we are going to rip). So, click on the **Choose...** button and select the CD audio track.

VLC should then take us back to the input window, with the audio track already selected (under **Select a stream**; in my case, this is `file://localhost/Volumes/Audio%20CD/...`). So we just need to click on the **Next** button.

We now have to select the destination audio codec in the **Transcode** window, so we should select the **Transcode audio** checkbox and then select the MP3 codec, with a bitrate of 128 kb/s (the frequency of the PCM original file, 44,100 Hz, will be retained) as we saw in the table of reference values in this chapter.

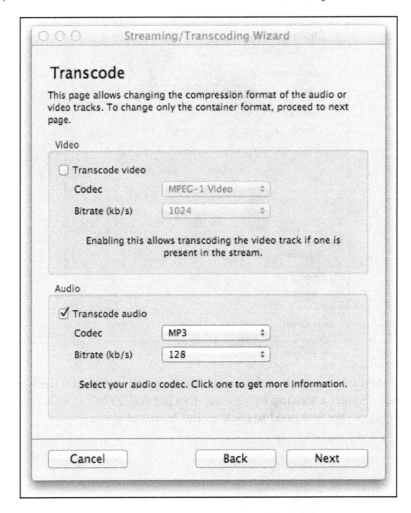

After clicking on **Next**, the **Encapsulation format** window is displayed. Here, we should select **RAW**.

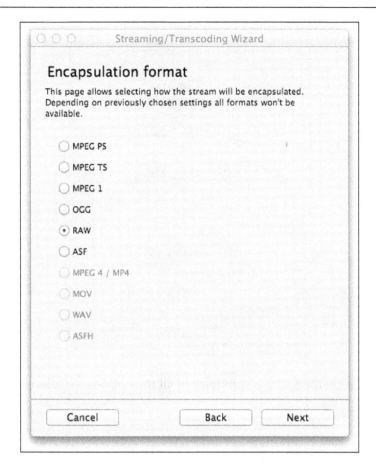

After clicking on the **Next** button again, we need to choose where to save the file.

1. Click on the **Choose** button.
2. Browse to the destination folder.
3. Add a filename and specify the file extension .mp3.

4. Click on the **Next** button.

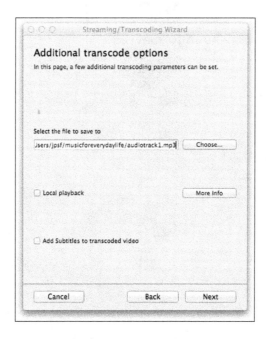

Finally, we are presented with a summary of all the options we selected with the wizard.

After we click on the **Finish** button, the transcoding will start and the wizard will disappear. The VLC player will look the same, and although nothing appears to be happening, the transcoding process is working in the background. We can recognize this in two ways—by listening to your CD drive working (if it's working, the transcoding is still going on), or by looking at the progress bar at the bottom of the VLC Media Player window, as shown in the following screenshot:

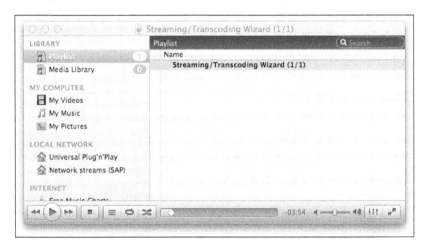

When the time value reaches 00:00, it's done. Now that we have some audio to work with, it's time to start the editing!

Creating and editing audio using Audacity

Audacity (http://audacity.sourceforge.net) is a free software utility for audio recording and editing that works on several platforms. It can be used to make high-quality recordings with a microphone (or other sources), easy editing and mixing of different sounds, mixing speech and music just like a real radio station, adding different audio effects, and all of this using a multitrack interface, where each audio file is assigned to a different track, which is a kind of layer that we can edit individually. The majority of the music that we listen to is recorded using this multitrack method, meaning that each instrument is recorded separately and then merged into a single audio file for playback.

At the time of writing this book, Audacity 2.0.3 is the latest release, and hence all of the procedures used in this chapter refer to this release. The latest release may differ in terms of the GUI and may have some additional functionality.

We will now see how we can use Audacity for some common procedures in audio creation and editing, such as:

- Slicing a track
- Capturing audio from a microphone
- Remixing audio

The following section lists some of the common activities in Audacity, and should be mostly read as a reference when you need to perform one of the described actions.

Audacity's interface has several toolbars:

- **The control toolbar**: This has the most important tools for editing the audio tracks and controlling the playback and recording
- **The meter toolbar**: This indicates the input and output levels, so that we can get a visual indication of the levels, for example, if your microphone is very low, or if the final sound is too high
- **The mixer toolbar**: This has the control sliders for the output level (a standard volume indicator) and your input level (for example, increasing the volume of the microphone before or during the recording)
- **The edit toolbar**: This has the tools for cutting, copying, and pasting selections, in addition to trimming, silence generation, undo and redo, and zooming
- **The input/output selector**: This identifies the devices that work as audio input (microphone for example) and output (speakers, for example)
- **The playback speed control**: This controls the playback speed from zero to three times faster
- **The timeline**: This indicates the length of the recording or playback in minutes and seconds
- **The tracks**: These are the different sounds that are a part of the audio project

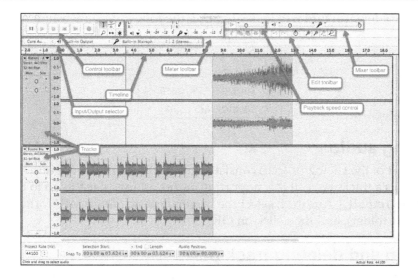

Let's start with the basic operation of slicing music tracks.

Slicing a track

Continuing our work in creating a soundtrack for the Tears of Steel movie trailer, the next step is to create slices of the music tracks that we extracted from the WIRED CD. As we want to create a limited video excerpt, we couldn't fit the entire music tracks, so we will have to cut out the parts that we don't want. This slicing is also useful in *Module 1, Music evolves*, where students have to create short audio clips from several music eras and post them as attachments in forum posts.

For slicing, we should start by creating a new audio project.

Creating a new audio project

To create audio clips from larger music files, the first thing to do is to create a new audio project. This means that we will have a folder where we can keep all of our files. So after opening Audacity, go to the **File** menu, click on **Save project as...**, and select a destination folder. A project file with the .aup extension will be created (in my case, I called it soundtrack) and a subfolder (soundtrack_data) will automatically be created by Audacity to contain all of the changes that we make to the original files. It's a good idea to create a folder in the destination folder, for the original music files that we will be using in the soundtrack project (I have called it music) and another one just for sound effects (I've called it fx).

Hence, the folder structure will look similar to the following screenshot:

Importing audio

The first part of the slicing process consists of importing a music file into the workspace as a track. We call this importing audio, and we need to go to the **File** menu, go to **Import | Audio…**, select the original music file (in MP3 format by now in our music folder), and then click on **OK**.

Selecting and deleting track parts

We have two options for deleting the parts of the music file that we are not interested in. The first is to use the **Selection** tool in the control toolbar, and then drag the mouse over the selection of the waveform that we wish to delete, finally pressing on the *Delete* key to delete it.

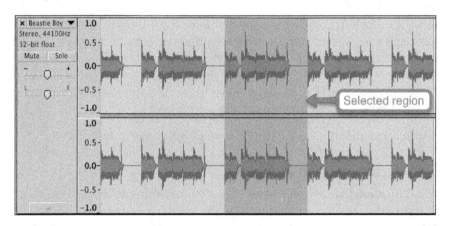

The second method is ideal for selecting an excerpt from the middle of the music file. In this method we use the **Trim** tool in the **Edit** toolbar. This will remove the audio regions before and after the excerpt that we select.

Fading in and fading out

If we remove parts of the track at the beginning and/or end of the music file, it can happen that if we play it now (using the control bar play button or by pressing Space bar), it starts and ends abruptly. Audacity has an option to make these smoother — the fade in and out effects.

To use these effects, we will first have to select a portion of the beginning of the excerpt, usually around three seconds. We can see this duration in the timeline and set it to more or less by using the **Zoom** tool. Then, after selecting around three seconds of music, go to **Effect | Fade In**, and it's done for this part.

We should apply the same principles to the end of the excerpt, in this case, using the **Fade Out** effect.

Exporting to MP3

Due to copyright issues, Audacity cannot export audio files to the MP3 format out of the box, so we will need to install an MP3 encoder called LAME, which is available free of cost.

1. Go to the LAME MP3 Encoder download page at `http://lame1.buanzo.com.ar/#lamewindl`.

2. Save the EXE or DMG file for our OS to our computer and install it. It should contain the encoder file. We should keep this file in a folder that we will not accidentally delete.

3. Open up Audacity. Go to the **Edit | Preferences...** and in the **Quality** tab, set the default rate to 44,100 Hz (CD quality). Also, in the **Libraries** tab, locate the encoder file file to allow Audacity to export files in the MP3 format (you will only need to do this once). After doing this, click on the **OK** button to go back to the project.

Finally, we should export our music selection to an MP3 file by going to **File | Export** and selecting the MP3 format, specifying some of the metadata. Our files will then be ready to Moodle! Note two things about this:

- We can use this procedure to convert another audio format to MP3, first opening it in Audacity and then exporting to MP3

- To save MP3 audio files with other rates and bitrates (for example, voice recordings), we should first click on the **Options** button in the **Export** dialog box and then export the result

Capturing audio from a microphone (line-in)

Capturing audio from a microphone (or any other input device) can be useful for many activities, such as:

- Adding audio comments to Moodle forums
- Recording an instrument
- Recording the audio that is playing through your speakers
- Converting old K7 recordings to digital audio

Combining music excerpts with voice comments can be interesting in our music course. In *Module 10, What's good music?*, students will act as music critics and create a collaborative database of CD reviews. These reviews will consist of a short text accompanied by their own voice comments, interleaved with excerpts from the CD that they've chosen to review.

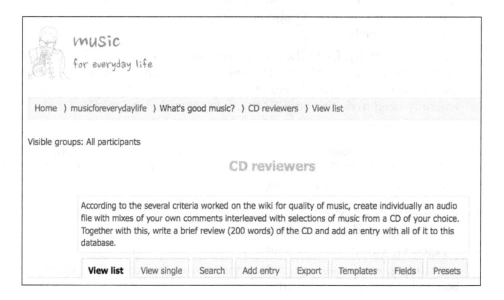

So let's have a look at how we can first capture our own voice, and later, remix it with music excerpts.

Selecting the audio input

In the **Input** device drop-down menu on Audacity's **Input/Output selector**, the first thing to choose is the microphone as the input source. When we click on the **Record** button, Audacity will capture whatever sound is coming from our microphone.

ment = segment

Tips for microphone capturing

For a better voice recording, most soundcards have an option to amplify the microphone signal. This option differs depending upon the operating system that we are using (Windows Vista, Windows XP, or Linux), so the best thing to do is to perform a web search with the keywords `mic + boost + operating system`. We will be able to find guidance for your operating system very easily. For Mac, the amplification of the built-in microphone should be enough.

Before we start recording, there's one last thing to keep in mind – the input volume. There is a potential problem that might arise from talking too close to the microphone – the sound can get distorted and the recording will be difficult to hear (we usually call this clipping or distortion). Another potential problem is the input being too low, and the recording will again be difficult to hear. The best way to control this is to monitor the input levels by clicking on the microphone levels in the **Meter** toolbar and start talking to the microphone. If the levels are low (the red bar is short), we can adjust the input volume in the **Mixer** toolbar. So, if you have a microphone or other input source attached to your computer, you will be able to control the level of the audio before you start recording.

The input meter shows us many things: the left and right channels input level (the **L** and **R** bars), the average audio level (in a lighter red) and the peak audio level (in a darker red), and the blue peak hold lines at the right of the level bars showing the maximum audio level achieved in the last three seconds.

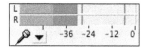

A good reference point while controlling the input volume in the Mixer toolbar is the rightmost edge of the bar for the loudest audio level (and the average below that, of course). So we should try talking (especially in the parts we think will be louder), check the peaks, and control the input volume with the input volume slider in the Meter bar.

Recording voice

Finally, we can click on the **Record** button. Every time we click on this button (after stopping the previous recording), a new track is created. If we are doing a retake because something went wrong in our first take, we can remove the previous track by clicking on the cross in the upper corner of the track to close it.

Amplifying sound

If we still have an amplification problem, the solution is to amplify an audio selection. After selecting the section of the recording that you want to amplify, go to **Effect** | **Amplify...** and increase the amplification (dB). Make sure that the waveform doesn't reach the top (value 1.0). For example, in the following screenshot, refer to the waveforms to the left of the first red bar and you can see a clipped recording. In the middle is a balanced recording, and on the right of the second red bar is a recording with a low input level.

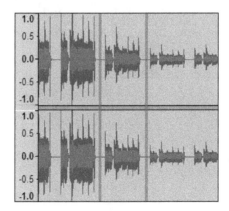

Importing audio tracks

We can import audio tracks to the project by going to the menu and selecting **Project** | **Import** | **Audio**. This can be useful for importing music tracks and alternating them with voice comments.

Moving tracks in the timeline

To reorder tracks in the timeline, we can use the **Time shift** tool in the **Control** toolbar. By left-clicking on an audio track and dragging it to the left or right, we can position it where we want it in the timeline.

Reducing the MP3 file size of voice recordings

After we have all of the voice and music clips sequenced, we can export the result as an MP3 file. In the case of voice-only projects, and if it is not a special voice recording, we can save a lot of disk space as follows. Before we start recording, we should go to the **Quality** tab in the **Preferences** tab in Audacity and choose the default sample rate as 11,025 Hz, the default sample format as 16 bits, and in **Options** in the **Export** dialog, select a bitrate of 48 kbps. Finally, export the project to MP3.

Remixing audio

Remixing audio is everywhere in the digital world. In TV and radio shows, Audio CDs, DVD movies, all of these use some degree of remixed audio from several sources.

We are now going to start mixing our music and sound effects, for the movie trailer soundtrack.

Cut, copy, and paste

With the **Selection** tool, we can cut, copy, and paste audio selections in the same way as in a text processor with regular text. But now, instead of paragraphs, the concept to use is a new audio track that is created to insert the copied or cut slices. We can then move these slices around and sequence them as we saw previously with the **Time shift** tool.

Creating a new audio track

We can create an empty new audio track for our project. For this, we just need to go to **Tracks | Add New | Audio Track**. Here we can cut and paste or copy and paste the selections in it.

Creating volume gradients using the Envelope tool

Editing the amplitude envelope lets us change the volume of a track, gradually over time, by adding a number of control points to the track. Each control point sets the amplitude (volume) at that point in time. This can be as low as zero, and as high as 150 percent of the normal maximum volume, and the volume is interpolated smoothly between the points.

The following screenshot shows a track for which an amplitude envelope was created with the help of the **Envelope** tool.

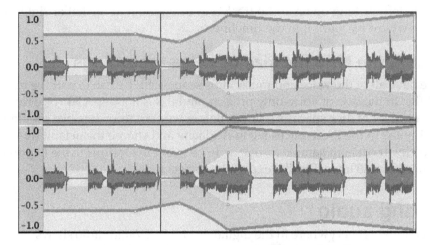

In the preceding screenshot, there are several control points identified by small squares. Each control point has up to four handles, arranged vertically. The top and bottom handles are positioned at the target volume and the middle handles are positioned a quarter screen below, giving us a way to move the envelope above the **1.0** level.

To create a new control point, just click. To move a point, just drag. To remove a point, we have to click on it and drag it onto an area outside of the track, and then release the mouse button.

Converting text to speech using Voki

Converting text to speech is a way that screen readers use to help visually impaired people to use the Web. It can also be used to add audio to forums; for example, if we don't have a microphone available, we can even create avatars with different looks and voices. We will use it in a role-play game in a forum by using Voki in our course module *Module 10, What's good music?*, where students will have to create a character with its own voice that gives arguments to defend a music genre.

Voki (`http://www.voki.com`) allows us to create avatars that can talk either with our own voice or by converting text to speech.

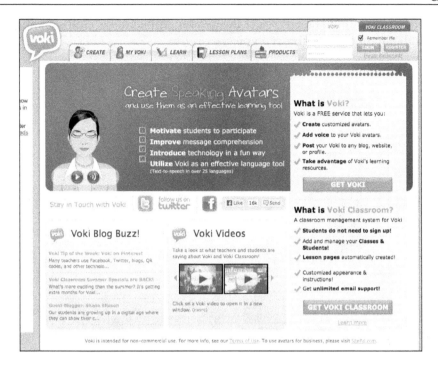

The voices that are available in Voki are not perfect if we want to have something very formal, but it can be really fun for students (for example, matching a silly voice to a serious character).

To start using Voki, we have to create a new account and then on the **Voki For My Site** tab, click on the **Create A New Voki** button.

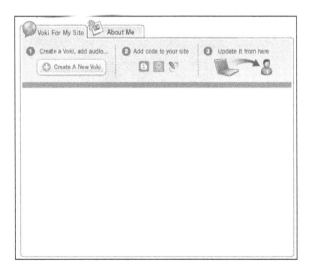

We can customize our character, select the gender, appearance, clothes, bling, background, and of course, give it a voice.

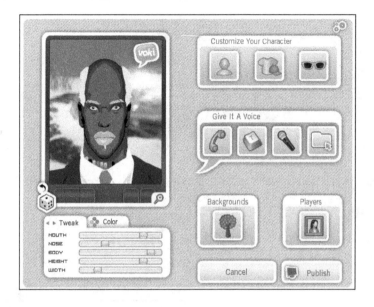

Giving voice to an avatar

After selecting an avatar's appearance, let's try giving it a voice by using **text-to-speech** (the second icon from the left). We have to type the text in the form, select the accent and voice alternatives, and click on the **Play** button.

Note that we can also record directly from a phone, a microphone, or can upload an audio file.

After we have finished giving voice to our avatar, click on the **Done** button and then on the **Publish** button. A pop up will ask us to name the scene. Once we name it, the avatar is ready to be used. We can now embed it in Moodle by using the given code.

The result will be similar to the following screenshot:

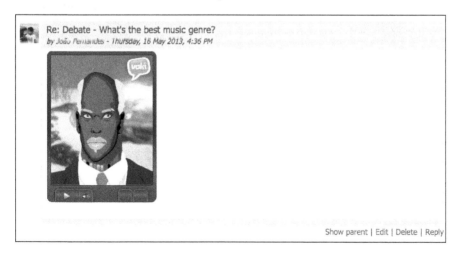

Podcasting using PodOmatic

A podcast can be thought of as a radio show that is distributed on the Web, just for subscribers. This means that when we, as authors, create a new episode, our subscribers automatically receive it on their computer or an iPod (the Apple device that gave the name to this distribution mechanism) connected to the computer via a kind of synchronization process. Thus, a podcast is not the usual concept of radio where a station is continually broadcasting. In addition, podcasts can be audio- or video-based (for example, `http://itunes.stanford.edu`). We also need a player to automatically download podcasts, for example Podfy (`http://www.podfy.com`).

And with PodOmatic, we are going to create podcasts, and we don't even need a player.

PodOmatic (`http://www.podomatic.com`) is an online community that loves podcasting. We can create our own podcasts online without the need to install any extra software. As an example of a podcast, we can create an audio magazine of what's going on in the course. We can talk about some of the activities that are being done, some things that we learned, and of course, some songs that we've been listening to.

After creating a new account, in the homepage we need to click on the **New episode** button.

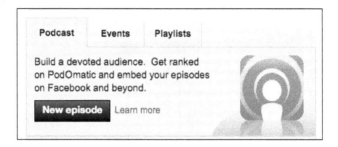

We can then fill in the name of the episode and the description, and click on the **Save & Continue** button. A new dialog will appear, this time for adding the content of our podcast's episode. We can upload files from our computer or even record directly by using our webcam or microphone. Let's see as an example how to upload files. First, we should click on the **Upload a file** link.

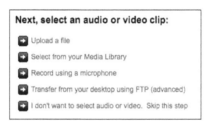

Next, we should click on the **Select some files** button and then select the required files from your computer:

We then have to select a photo for the episode (600 px x 600 px size recommended), add some tags, and click on the **Save & Continue** button when done.

In the following example, I added a *Tears of Steel* movie picture:

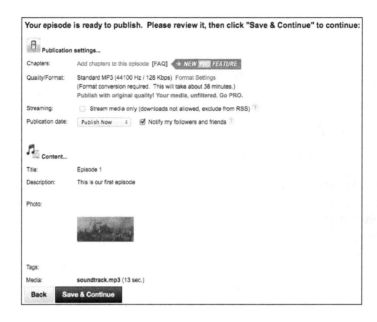

To add this podcast to Moodle, we need to click on the **Embed** tab in the episode's page as shown in the following screenshot:

Finally, we need to copy the embed code and paste it in Moodle. We can also add a link to the podcast on the course so that others can subscribe to it.

Summary

In this chapter, we focused on tasks for the Moodle integration of sound and music elements. The resources created will make information available in improved ways to students and will also get them engrossed in creating audio artifacts, such as slices, remixes, voice recordings, text to speech, and podcasts. We used several tools to achieve this, especially Audacity, VLC Media Player, PodOmatic, and Grooveshark, and we also saw where to find free sounds and music.

Now that we can do some things with audio, why not try video? From stop motion to video editing in general, to movies made out of photos, and to online TV channels, it's all in the next chapter.

4
Video

This chapter will be dedicated to creating and editing videos for our course, from grabbing excerpts of video DVDs and making screencasts that record our screen actions to proper video editing and stop motion animation or even broadcasting an online TV. We will also learn how to download videos from online video sharing services and convert these to other formats.

In this chapter we will cover the following topics:

- Using a set of software tools for common procedures in video creation, editing, and broadcasting
- Publishing and downloading videos from online video sharing services
- Converting a video format into several others and vice versa
- Integrating video in Moodle

Finding free videos online

Wikimedia Commons and the Internet Archive (for example, `http://www.archive.org/details/moviesandfilms`) are usually a safe option for downloading and using videos in our video projects. Although these are very useful, they are not the only services available; we can find many others with particular interest to teachers and trainers. YouTube (`http://www.youtube.com`) is well known and has lots of useful stuff, but there are many others.

However, before we check reference websites where we can find interesting videos and embed them in our courses, let's first have a look at the basics of video formats.

The basics of video formats

With video, things start to get complicated concerning formats. Rates, bitrates, codecs, formats, sizes, frame rates, and on top of this, all the audio varieties can overwhelm us. We should know some of these formats:

- **AVI with Xvid or DivX**: AVI is a common video format using the Xvid or DivX codecs, giving a good quality/file size for movies converted from DVDs.

- **MPEG-2**: MPEG-2 is a DVD video format. If we explore a DVD filesystem, it contains VOB files, which are containers of video, audio, subtitles, and menus in this format.

- **MPEG-4**: MPEG-4 is now a common format for online video used by YouTube.

- **MOV**: MOVE is an Apple multimedia file format. It also contains videos, along with other information such as subtitles.

- **OGG**: OCG is an open source format that is worth checking.

- **WMV**: Windows Media Video is a format developed by Microsoft with a good quality-to-size ratio. It can be edited and exported easily in Windows operating systems and uploaded to online video sharing services.

Remember that audio is a very important part of video and sometimes, when we use cheap cameras, we can have a good video and bad audio quality. We can solve this by either buying a proper digital camcorder or capturing the audio separately and mixing it with the video later on, with video editing software.

Webcams, mobile phones, and digital cameras use a certain video resolution (and also formats but that is another story) that reflects the size of the video in pixels (160 x 120, 320 x 240, 640 x 480, 720 x 576, and so on); so keep in mind that for screen playback, a size of 640 x 480 or above is the best. Whenever possible choose this one, as it will also work well with online video services if you want to share it. Now let's see where to find some nice videos for our Moodle courses.

Instructables

On Instructables (`http://www.instructables.com`), we can find and share short tutorial videos on how to do things, from cooking to art and from origami to robots.

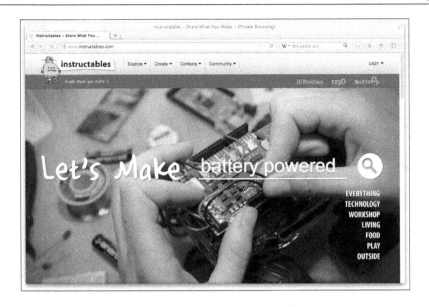

TED Talks

TED Talks (`http://www.ted.com/talks`) are short, usually 20-minute conferences, by thinkers and doers from around the world, such as scientists, philanthropists, artists, philosophers, and many others. The TED Talks motto is *Ideas worth spreading*.

Vimeo

Vimeo (`https://vimeo.com`) is an online video sharing service created by filmmakers that has many interesting videos with a focus on image quality.

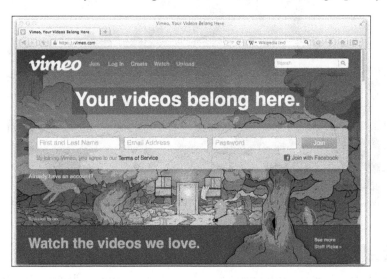

TrueTube

TrueTube (`http://www.truetube.co.uk`) is a place for debating social issues, such as culture, ethics, environment, society or economy. The main idea is to have young people discussing and posting their videos and views. It also makes lesson plans on these themes available.

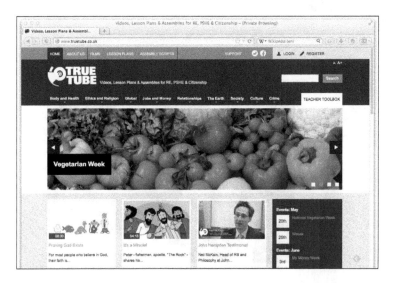

Academic Earth

On Academic Earth (`http://academicearth.org`), we can find many lectures from top scholars around the world, including those from the Khan Academy (`https://www.khanacademy.org`).

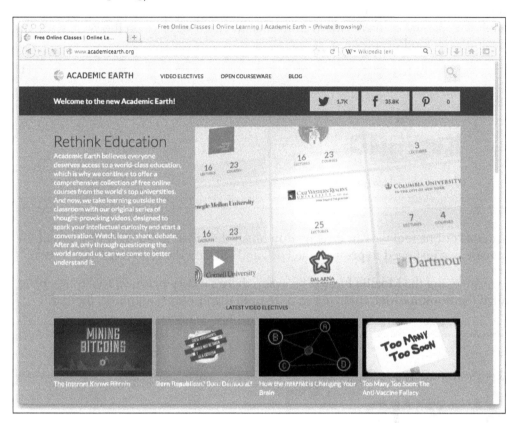

Downloading online videos

Sometimes, it can be useful to download videos from online video sharing services if we want to show them at a time when we don't have an Internet connection or the service is blocked by a firewall, for example, in a school. There are some online tools that make this download easy. With KeepVid (`http://keepvid.com`), we can download and convert videos from several video services on the Web, without installing any kind of software.

With this online tool we can directly download the video in the MPEG-4 format. In this case, we just need to provide the URL and click on the **DOWNLOAD** button.

If we are using the Mozilla Firefox browser, there's a very practical tool in KeepVid, called the **Bookmarklet**, that we can drag onto the Firefox bookmarks toolbar.

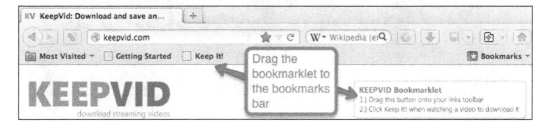

When we are watching a video and want to download it, we just need to click on this bookmark and the download links will be automatically created and presented to us.

To download the video, we just need to right-click on the download link and choose the **Save link as...** option.

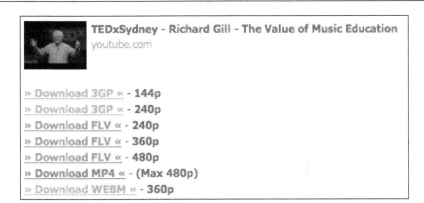

Creating videos quickly and cheaply

With so many digital cameras in the market and the prices of storage going down, the tools to create and edit videos are now more accessible to everyone. We will have a look at some techniques in the following sections, namely:

- Grabbing video selections from DVDs with VLC
- Editing videos using Windows Live Movie Maker
- Creating photo slideshows (videos made of photos) with YouTube
- Creating an online TV with Google Hangouts and YouTube
- Creating screencasts (screen recordings) with Google Hangouts
- Creating a stop motion movie with JellyCam

Let's begin by using the work of others in our creations and extracting video selections from DVDs.

Grabbing video selections from DVDs

Extracting video selections from a DVD can be really useful, for example, if we want to edit a video that we have created with a digital camera that records onto DVD discs, or extract a selection from a regular DVD. In our course, in *Module 3, Music and media*, students are asked to create a movie trailer for the *Tears of Steel* movie (as we saw earlier), so they will be required to extract several slices from the original DVD.

This is a Creative Commons licensed movie, so we don't have many copyright restrictions, but note that these instructions will still work with copyright-protected DVDs (which includes most DVDs that you buy). Also, be careful that you are not breaking any laws by doing so. Refer to *Chapter 8, Common Multimedia Issues in Moodle*, for further guidance on this.

After putting the DVD in the computer's DVD player, let's open the VLC **Streaming/ Exporting** wizard again, as we saw with the CD ripping. Go to **File | Open Disc...**, select the title we want to open. DVD movies are organized according to titles, which are the main video files (Title 1 is usually the main movie and Title 2 could be, for example, some extra material—most of the time, there is no need to change the subtitles or audio tracks' values), and these titles are made out of chapters. The best thing to do is to open the disc in VLC (**File | Open Disc... | DVD**) and try the title numbers before performing the transcoding, to see if VLC plays the title that we intend to rip.

Then, let's select the checkbox that says **Streaming/Saving:** and click on the **Settings...** button.

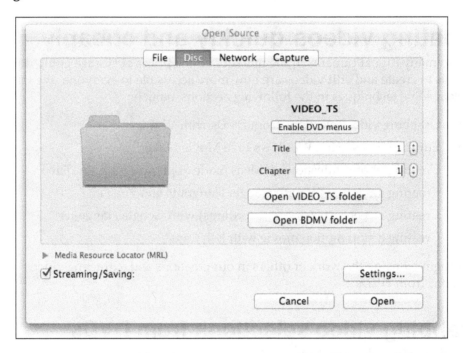

In the next window, we should now check the **File** field at the top and then click on **Browse...** and select where we want to save the file. We should also add an extension to the file, in this case, .avi. Then, in **Encapsulation format**, we must select **MPEG TS**.

Do not choose either of the options shown, that is, **Video** or **Audio** under **Transcoding options**.

Then click on **OK**.

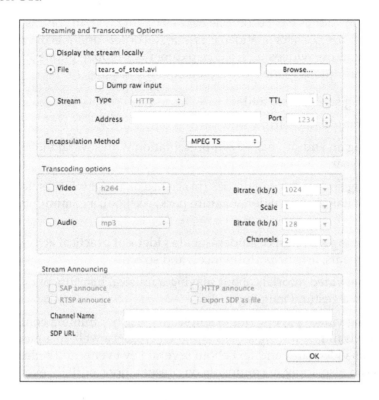

After we click on the Next button on the initial **Disc** screen, VLC will start converting the file and we will see this in the status bar. The time will advance as the process continues and depending on our CPU, it can be faster or slower. Either way, as we are not transcoding (converting it to another video format), the process will be a quick one (probably less than 10 minutes for the entire *Tears of Steel* movie).

The resulting files in this kind of process can be quite large. This is because we are not using any encoding of the original file (remember VOB files that make up a DVD are MPEG-2 encoded), making the process faster but demanding more in terms of the amount of disk space required. Each minute of video will need around 50 MB of disk space, meaning that the 12-minute movie we are extracting will need approximately 600 MB! We are using this process because it is the best way to work with the video in a video editing software application, in this case, Windows Movie Maker (something we will see right away). Later on, after editing it with this tool, we will transcode the final video to the MPEG-4 format, which can save us some disk space.

Editing videos using Windows Movie Maker

Editing video nowadays has become as easy as editing text. In contrast to the time when we had to use scissors or Video Cassette Recorders and lots of cables, we can now film and edit raw videos with a cheap camera or mobile phone and a few clicks, with great contributions to the education field, for example:

- Debating scenes from a film.

- Publishing a study trip video.

- Creating an end-of-year school presentation with several video clips from the school year.

- Creating simple documentaries (in science or social sciences, for example about a national or regional nature park, a school, a community issue, and so on).

- Organizing a contest of student-made videos of practical activities (science experiments, artistic performances, and so on).

- Creating video tutorials about playing a musical instrument or, for example, to teach a gestural language.

- Creating video "papers", for example, in a teacher training context, where a trainee is filmed during a class and then creates a web document where he embeds video clips and text about several key events and reflects on them. This can also apply to comments on presentations or daily events in general.

We will now see how we can make this kind of video using Windows Movie Maker, starting first by creating a two-and-a-half minutes trailer of the movie *Tears of Steel* that we have ripped previously, and adding a new soundtrack to it.

Windows Movie Maker is an easy-to-use, free video editing software that comes with Windows. The advantage of this kind of software (and its equivalent in Mac OS, iMovie) is that it usually comes with the operating systems of the computers in schools, so it's easy to start working with. I've chosen this software and not iMovie because Windows Movie Maker is more widely spread and because there is no free or open source software that can match it unfortunately (in terms of interface, functionality, and simplicity). So we will have to stick to the Windows solution. Some of the processes are common in Windows Movie Maker and in other video editing software, so it is hoped that they will also be helpful for Mac and Linux users. To install it, just go to `http://windows.microsoft.com/en-us/windows/get-movie-maker-download` and follow the instructions.

Creating a project

After we open Windows Movie Maker, the first thing that we need to do is create a project. Just like in Audacity, this application organizes several elements (videos, sound files, images, titles, and transitions) in one file, the so-called project file, with the .wlmp extension. So we can first create a folder in our computer, with the following subfolders: audio, video, and images and then in Windows Movie Maker, go to **File | Save** project as in the previously created folder and save the project with a name of your choice (just make sure that you don't use spaces or uppercase, just plain text with underscores replacing the spaces—this is a good practice if we want to share these files in Moodle later). The best practice in video editing (and editing in general) is to have all the files for the project in a single folder, as it makes it easier to not lose our sources when we back up our data, and makes it easy to transfer the project and all of its files to another workstation.

Importing multimedia – starting with video

We will now import the main video file that we have extracted from the DVD into the Movie Maker project. After moving the original .avi file that we extracted with VLC to the video subfolder of the project, we have to click on the active area on the right-hand side of the main window application and browse for it.

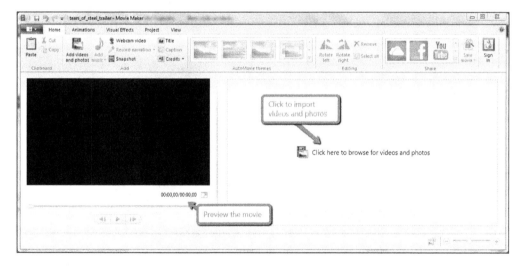

Splitting

Just like in Audacity, we can use the Space bar to start and stop the playback of the movie file in the previewing area. This is very practical, because we can find the right moment where we want to split the video and just press Space bar instead of using the mouse and clicking on the **Pause** button. We can also fine-tune our splitting frame by using either the buttons in the monitoring window, or the *J* and *L* keys for the previous and next frames respectively.

To split the video clip, after selecting the exact moment of splitting, we have to click on the **Split** button or press the *M* key. We will get another clip on the right of the main application window that we can later split or remove.

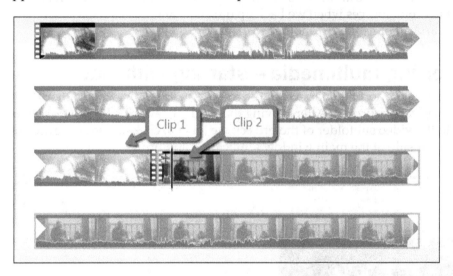

Inserting animations and visual effects

Inserting animations and visual effects is as easy as selecting the clip to which we want to apply them and then the desired effect. If we click on the **Animations** or **Visual Effects** tab in the ribbon, we get thumbnails of the several effects that are available to us. If we click on each of them, we can preview it in the monitor by clicking on the **Play** button or by pressing the Space bar.

We can try some of the transitions and effects, specially the **Cross Dissolve, Fade Out, To Black**, and **Fade In, From Black**. We can add multiple effects to the same clip.

To remove a transition, we just need to select the clip and then the **No effect/No transition** box in the respective ribbon.

Inserting a title at the beginning of a clip

To add a title at the beginning of a clip, go to the ribbon and select **Title** in the **Home** tab. There are many options we can go through, such as the font, size, color, transparency, effects, and others.

Inserting an image at the end of the movie

Movie Maker also allows us to insert images, which will be displayed for a certain amount of time. For that we just have to go the **Home** tab, click on the **Add videos and photos** button, and select the image. It will be added as a clip to the main window. If we click on it, we can change its duration in seconds in the ribbon.

There are a couple of things to keep in mind when we add images to a movie. One of them would be the size of the picture in pixels. Its size should be at least the same as that of the video or, if larger, keep the same proportions. This will avoid distortions and loss of quality in the final movie. We can also add visual effects to images.

Removing the original soundtrack and inserting a new one

Despite the fact that Movie Maker has a narration option, the best thing to do is to capture voice and remix it with the rest of the music and sound effects in Audacity, and then import it to Movie Maker and define it as the movie soundtrack. One of the reasons for this is that Movie Maker only allows one audio track; so if we wanted to add voice with background music, that would be a problem. Another reason is that you cannot control the quality of the voice recording and mixing in Movie Maker as you can in Audacity.

To add a new soundtrack that will replace the clips' soundtrack, go to the **Home** tab, click on the **Add music** button, and select the audio file. A new row will be added to the clips. If we click on it, we are presented with some options such as **Fade in:** and **Fade out:**.

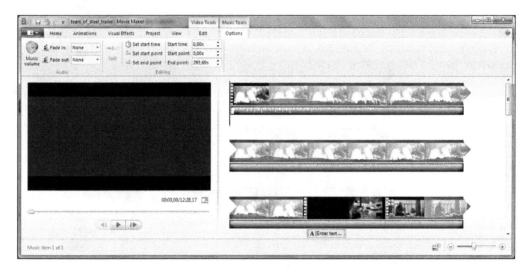

Saving the edited movie

To get the best quality possible, the export format for the completed trailer should be AVI. But we have already seen that this format is space-consuming, and as we want to send the video to YouTube, Movie Maker is ready for that. On the **Home** tab, click on the **Save movie** button, select the **YouTube** option, name your movie, and finally, click on the **Save** button.

Moodle it!

We have two ways of adding a video to Moodle. The first is to send the video files to the course files, later linking to it. The other is to upload the video to an online video service and later embed it in Moodle.

Uploading video directly to Moodle

Moodle, as we saw, has several multimedia plugins that automatically recognize a link to a multimedia file, such as a video, and automatically embed a player. If we upload the video in the YouTube format (MPEG-4 with the H.264 codec) to our course, it will play it in the browser window, thanks to Moodle's multimedia plugins.

Uploading videos to YouTube

Uploading our videos (including our students' videos) to a service such as YouTube has several advantages:

- If we don't have much space on our Moodle server, this will not load it with more files, particularly a video that is usually associated with large file sizes

- If we have many students trying to watch the same video in Moodle's files area, this will affect the server's performance

- As it uses the Flash or HTML5 video player, problems of different formats, players, and operating systems are solved

- If we publish it on these online services, other people can see and comment on it (this could be an advantage, depending on what we want; however, we can make some videos private)

We will now see how to send the published video to YouTube.

After we create an account in YouTube (through a Google Account), we should set up our channel page.

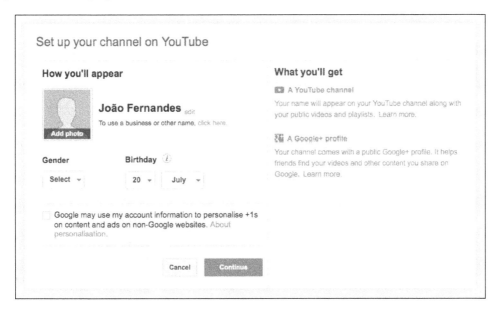

After clicking on **Continue**, we are taken to our channel page. This is where we will manage our videos, playlists, and other settings that will be of use while setting an online TV later in the chapter.

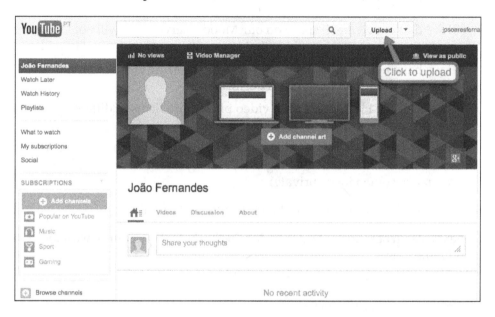

After we click on the **Upload** button, we need to click on **Select files to upload** or drag-and-drop the file from our computer to the active area of the screen on the left.

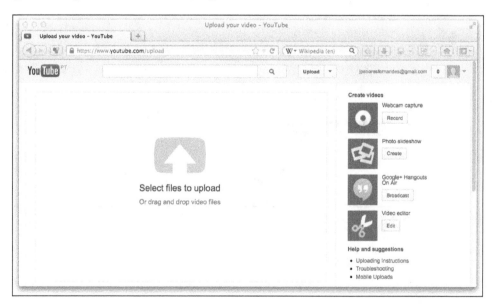

The next steps are to wait for the video to upload, fill in some information about it, and select the privacy options (whether we want the video to be public or private — the second option can be useful if we are concerned about e-safety, refer to *Chapter 8, Common Multimedia Issues in Moodle* for this).

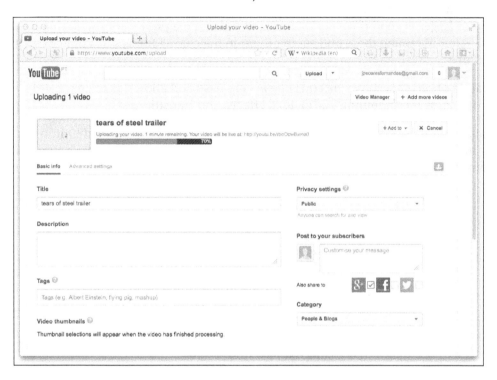

It will take some time until the video is ready but then, as we saw in *Chapter 1, Getting Ready for Multimedia in Moodle*, we will just need to use the embed code associated with the video to add it to Moodle and show our trailer to everyone.

Creating a photo slideshow using YouTube

Stories made out of photos are a good way to describe an event, make a presentation, or create a storyboard for a movie made out of scenes. In our course, in *Module 5, Being a musician*, every student will have to build a presentation of his/her favorite artist, based on some photos of their performances, albums, or daily life. I will use as an example António Carlos Jobim, the great Brazilian bossa nova composer who left a great part of his work available to the public after his death at `http://www.jobim.org`.

A good way to start a photo slideshow project is to create a folder for the project and subfolders for the photos (for example, based on the periods of the life of the artist and/or types of images that we have gathered, such as CD covers, photos, or screenshots). Remember that the photos should have approximately the same quality and at least a minimum size in pixels according to the desired photo story size (640 x 480 or larger is good if we are planning to publish the photo story with this size or less). After obtaining these and saving them in the correct folders, it's time to go to YouTube.

Creating photo slideshows in YouTube is very easy and allows us to create videos out of photos by combining audio, text, effects, and transitions.

So again, after we go to our YouTube channel and click on the **Upload** button (as we saw in the previous section), we should now click on the **Create** button below the **Photo slideshow** label on the right of the active area for drag-and-drop.

Uploading photos

Now we should select **Upload photos** on the left and drag-and-drop the pictures that we want to add to the photo slideshow to the active area on the screen.

We can reorder the pictures by dragging-and-dropping the thumbnails in the desired order.

Source: Instituto Antonio Carlos Jobim (2013). m01f026, m01f046, m01f049, m01f054, p37f011, p61f028, p61f054. Retrieved June 1, 2013, from http://www.jobim.org

After clicking on the Next button, we are taken to the basic photo slideshow editor. If we want to make one using a quick template, that's the way to go, so we would just need to select the slide duration, slide effect, and transitions between the photos and an audio track from a collection provided by YouTube and hit **Upload**. Instead, we will use **Advanced editor** and work some more details.

Adding background music

In **Advanced editor** we have access to more editing options, including a timeline view, audio tracks, transitions between photos, text on photos, titles, and photo effects.

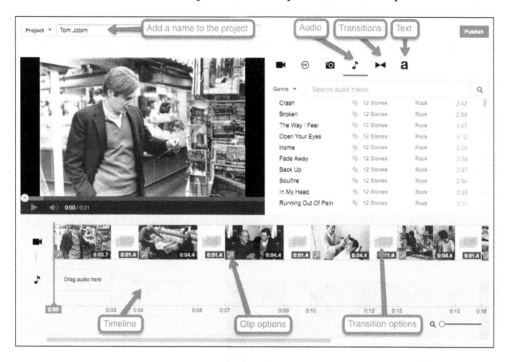

Let's begin by adding a soundtrack to the slideshow. In the Audio option in the top menu, we can search by genre an audio track from a long list of songs made available by YouTube. After selecting the song (we can preview it by hitting the Play button to the left of the song title), we just need to add it to the timeline's audio track either by dragging it there or clicking on the plus button on the right of the song title.

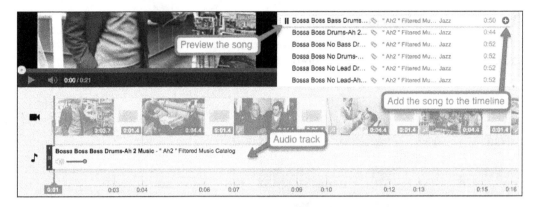

Adding transitions

By default, the basic editor adds cross-fade transitions between all the photos. If we want to change the transition effect, in the Transitions item of the top menu there are many to choose from. After choosing one, we just drag it onto where we want it in the timeline. We can also change its duration clicking with the mouse on the gray bar on the left or right of the transition and dragging it onto the desired duration.

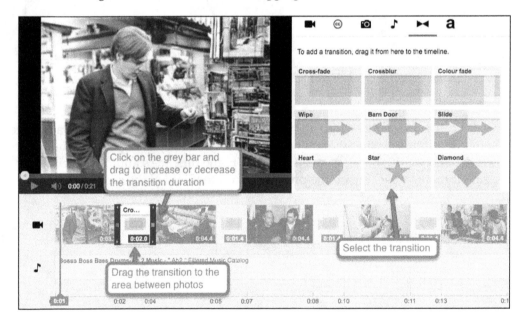

Adding titles

To add a title to our slideshow, we should click on the Text item of the top menu and select one of the templates, dragging it onto the right place in the timeline. Then, with the mouse over it, we should click on the **a** button to edit the title text.

Adding text to single photos

Besides titles to the slideshow, we can also add text to single photos. Then, with the mouse over the photo in the timeline, we should click on the **a** button to edit the photo's text.

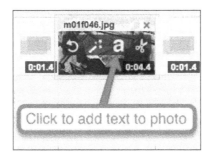

Adding effects to single photos

The same applies for adding effects to single photos. With the mouse over the photo in the timeline, we just need to click on the Wand button.

Finally, we just need to select the special effect and hit **Done**.

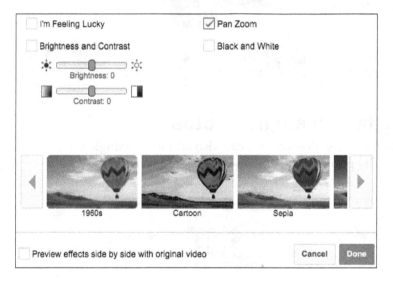

Publishing the photo slideshow

Finally, it's time to publish the photo slideshow and we're done! The slideshow will show up as a regular video in our channel page, so we can embed it in Moodle as we have seen before.

Creating an online TV using Google Hangouts and YouTube

Who would have guessed that we would live a time when anyone can make his/her own TV station with a computer, an Internet connection, and a cheap camera? And you can ignore the camera if you wish? With so many videos on the Web, it's really simple to get the raw material for your programming. Imagine a TV in our Moodle course with several programs, with live news directly from a webcam and videos made by you or by others who are part of this programming, and you will have an idea of what am I talking about. And you can set it up in 15 minutes. Yes, 15 minutes!

I can imagine 100 ways that we could use this in a school and in Moodle in particular to broadcast:

- A live school event, such as a school play
- Old school events, such as a history of our school
- Classes roleplaying, games in physical education classes, science experiments, and so on
- Shows made by students and teachers
- Meetings, workshops, and club activities
- Online videos selected by teachers or students, something similar to a pick of the day

In our course, students will be required to create a course channel that will be available in a side block. They will be using Google Hangouts and YouTube again, and design all of it in a collective way. They will start by building a foundation document for the station, with editorial standards and policies, the main theme, the programs, and the team's responsibilities using a Wiki to develop each of these aspects.

Google Hangouts (`http://www.google.com/hangouts`) is an online service that broadcasts live video conversations between Google users. This means that we can have live video in our YouTube channel for the world to see. For that, we will just need the Google Hangouts browser plugin and a webcam.

Setting up a Google Hangout

So, going again to our YouTube channel and clicking on the **Upload** button on the right menu, we can start broadcasting right away by clicking on **Broadcast** below **Google+ Hangouts On Air**.

We will be asked to connect our Hangout to Google+ and accept the terms of service, so we just need to follow the instructions. When all is set, we can start setting up our Hangout on air.

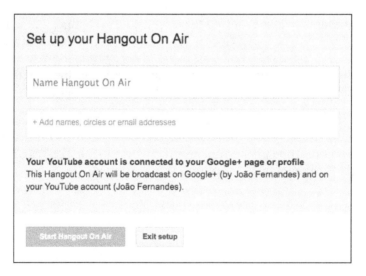

In the following screen, we are presented with a set of options on the left to broadcast our webcam, YouTube videos, our screen, or a remote screen. For now, let's just have a look at the webcam and YouTube videos.

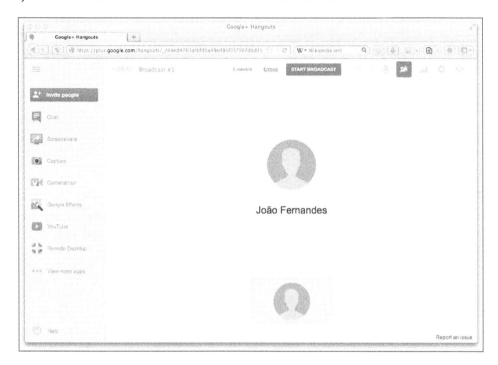

Broadcasting videos from a webcam

We can start broadcasting our webcam by clicking on the **START BROADCAST** button on the top menu. The information on air will show next to the title of the Hangout.

Inviting guests

We can also add guests to our broadcast by clicking on the **Invite people** button on the left menu.

Then, we can search by people on our contact list either by name or e-mail and when we're done, just hit the **Submit** button.

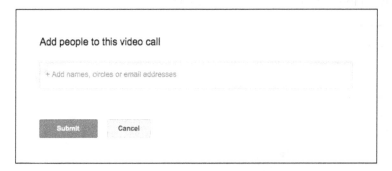

Broadcasting a guest webcam

When we have several people in a conversation with us, it can be useful to broadcast the webcam of one of our guests. For that, Hangouts has a **Cameraman** tool, accessible again from the menu on the left. When we click on it a window shows on the right and we can leave the default settings untouched.

When one or two guests join, they will be added automatically to the broadcast. More than that and as we kept the default Cameraman settings, they will all be muted when they join.

To change the broadcast status of a guest, there are three buttons to keep in mind below the thumbnail of our guest when we hover our mouse on it:

- Hide from broadcast: This turns off the the guest's video signal from the broadcast
- Mute: This turns off the guest's audio signal from the broadcast
- Eject: This removes the guest from the broadcast

Broadcasting YouTube videos

We can also add YouTube videos to our broadcast using the YouTube link on the left menu.

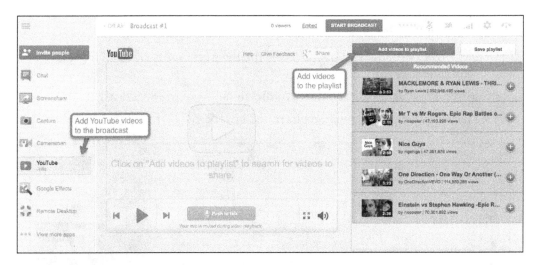

We then have to add or search videos for our broadcast by clicking on the **Add videos to playlist** button on the top right of the screen, entering your video search query or YouTube link, and clicking on the green plus button to add it to the playlist.

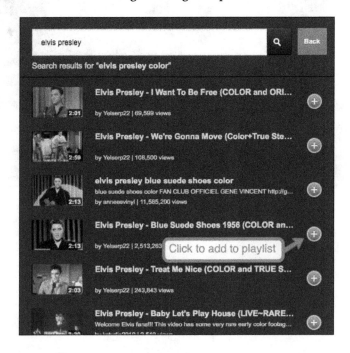

When we are ready, we can click on the **Back** button and we are taken back to the broadcast main window, showing the video that is now playing in our broadcast. If we want to comment on it using our microphone, we just need to hit the **Push to talk** button.

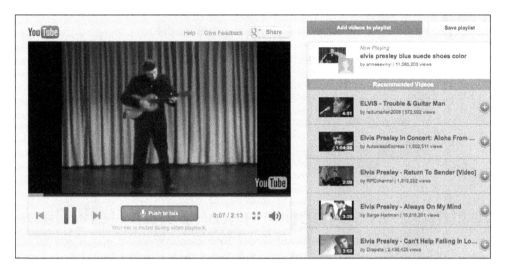

Remember that all of this will be automatically recorded for later on-demand watching.

Moodle it!

Next to the **Start Broadcasting** button, there's an Embed link that gives us either a URL or an embed code to add the online TV to our course. Simple as that.

Creating a screencast using Google Hangouts

Screencasts are recordings of screen actions and are very useful for showing procedures in a computer interface, as they reveal the mouse movements, clicking, typing, and more than that, audio comments. With Google Hangouts, it's really easy to create screencasts, just like the commented screenshots we saw previously.

Screencasts will be an important part of our course, as we will use them to create tutorials that support students in the use of the several tools used in the course activities. Hangouts is quite cool as it saves the screencast in YouTube, which we will then make available as a resource (link to a file) in our course.

Recording the screen with audio

Just before starting the screencast, we need to connect the microphone and headphones (the headset) to the audio ports in our computer, with the pink jack to the pink connector and the green jack to the green connector respectively.

After opening a new Hangout, we just have to perform the following steps:

1. Click on the **Screenshare** option in the left menu.
2. Select an application window already opened in our computer.
3. Start broadcasting.
4. Perform the actions with audio comments.
5. Stop broadcasting.

That's it!

Creating a stop motion movie with JellyCam

When I was a kid, I had a flipbook that when flipped, showed a woman getting up from bed. Page by page, the changes were too small to notice but from beginning to end, they meant the difference between being in bed and being up. In stop motion, this is the main concept—the accumulation of small changes of position in usually nonmoving objects that, when properly sequenced, simulate movement.

For the course in our module dedicated to music, dance, and emotions, one of the tasks will be to create a stop motion movie of a clay character that will be breakdancing. For this we will use JellyCam (`http://www.ticklypictures.com/shop/jellycam`). To start, we should perform the following steps:

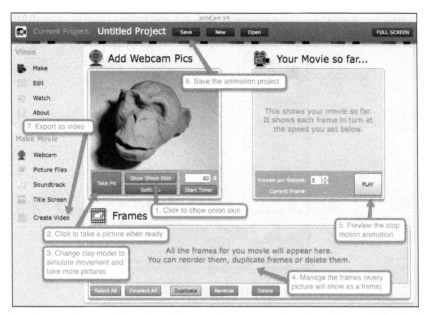

Source: fronx (2012), plasticine chimp [head] Retrieved June 5, 2013, from http://www.flickr.com/photos/
fronx/8266605549/

1. Connect your camcorder or webcam to the computer and then open
   JellyCam. The webcam image will show on the **Add Webcam Pics** window.

2. Activate the **Show Onion Skin** tool. This allows us to see the previous
   position of the object with a level of opacity a little bit below the next image
   to be captured by the camera, similar to a ghost of the previous frame.

3. Click on the **Take Pic** button. A frame will be added to the **Frames** window.

4. Change the clay model to simulate a small movement. Take a pic and repeat
   the process as many times as needed.

5. Manage the frames in the **Frame** window, delete those that didn't work well,
   or rearrange them as needed.

6. Click on the **Play** button to preview the frames animation. We can change the
   frames per second value to have smoother (higher value) or more robot-like
   movement (lower value).

7. Save the animation project.

8. Export the project as a video (the `.flv` format) clicking on the **Create
   Movie** link.

Finally, to add the movie to Moodle we could, for example, publish the final video to YouTube and embed it.

Summary

In this chapter, we focused on video production and editing, looking at different ways of using these in Moodle. We started by looking at the basics of video formats and places to find free video online, followed by ways of downloading videos from YouTube. We then looked at ways of extracting DVD selections for later editing, and how to create photo slideshows, screencasts, an online TV station, and a stop motion video. Exploring Google Hangouts and YouTube was a good introduction to online-based software (sometimes called webware), and in *Chapter 5, Understanding Web-based Applications and Other Multimedia Forms*, we will focus on the kind of tools that are very common these days and useful for teaching and learning. This concept of the Web as an operating system and web tools as social applications can be a nice metaphor for learning and can extend Moodle's possibilities, by giving students more tools for creating content and a space to reflect, discuss, and assess these creations.

5
Understanding Web-based Applications and Other Multimedia Forms

In this chapter, we will focus essentially on web-based applications for creating multimedia.

However, we will not look at blogs, wikis, or social networking sites that are usually referred to as web-based reference tools. Moodle already has these, so instead we will take a look at web applications that allows the easy creation, collaboration, and sharing of multimedia elements, such as interactive floor planners, online maps, timelines, and many others applications that are very easy to use, and that support different learning styles. Usually, I use Moodle as a school operating system and web apps as its social applications, to illustrate what I believe can be a very powerful way of using Moodle and the web for learning. Designing meaningful activities in Moodle gives students the opportunity to express their creativity by using these tools, and reflecting on the produced multimedia artifacts with both peers and teacher.

However, we have to keep in mind some issues of e-safety, backups, and licensing when using these online tools, usually associated with online communities. After all, we will have our students using them, and they will therefore be exposed to some risks. The last chapter of this book will deal with these issues.

By the end of this chapter, you will be able to:

- Use a set of free online software tools for common procedures in multimedia creation and sharing
- Create interactive multimedia artifacts for use in course delivery
- Integrate these multimedia artifacts in Moodle

Creating dynamic charts using Google Drive (Spreadsheets)

Assigning students in our Moodle course tasks such as preparing a studio budget in *Module 6*, *Spaces for music*, will require them to use a tool like Google Spreadsheets to present their plans to colleagues in a visual way.

Google Drive (`http://drive.google.com`) provides a set of online productivity tools that work on web standards and recreates a typical Office suite. We can make documents, spreadsheets, presentations, drawings, or forms.

To use Google Drive, we will need a Google account. After creating our account and logging in to Google Drive, we can organize the files displayed on the right side of the screen, add them to folders, tag them, search (of course, it's Google!), collaborate (imagine a wiki spreadsheet), export to several formats (including the usual formats for Office documents from Microsoft, Open Office, or Adobe PDF), and publish these documents online.

We will start by creating a new Spreadsheet to make a budget for a music studio which will be built during the music course, by navigating to **CREATE | Spreadsheet**.

Insert a chart

As in any spreadsheet application, we can add a title by double-clicking on **Untitled spreadsheet**, and then we add some equipment and cost to the cells:

After populating our table with values and selecting all of them, we should click on the Insert chart button.

The **Start** tab will show up in the **Chart Editor** pop up, as shown in the following screenshot:

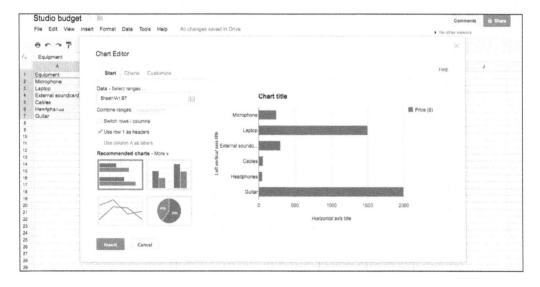

If we click on the **Charts** tab, we can pick from a list of available charts. Let's pick one of the pie charts.

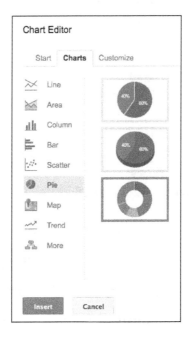

In the **Customize** tab, we can add a title to the chart, and change its appearance:

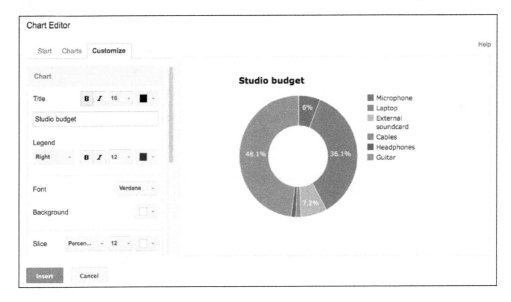

When everything is done, we can click on the **Insert** button, and the chart previewed in the **Customize** tab will be added to the spreadsheet.

Publish

If we click on the chart, a square will be displayed on the upper-right corner, and if we click on the drop-down arrow, we see a **Publish chart...** option, which can be used to publish the chart.

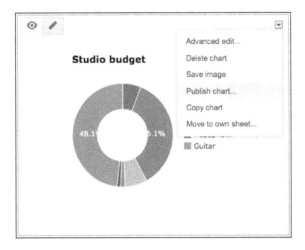

When we click on this option, we will be presented with two ways of embedding the chart, the first, as an interactive chart, and the second, as an image. Both change dynamically if we change the values or the chart in Google Drive. We should use the image code to put the chart on a Moodle forum, as we have seen in previous chapters.

Share, comment, and collaborate

Google Drive has the options of sharing and allowing comments and changes in our spreadsheet by other people. On the upper-right corner of each opened document, there are two buttons for that, **Comments** and **Share**.

To add collaborators to our spreadsheet, we have to click on the **Share** button and then add their contacts (for example, e-mail) in the **Invite people:** field, then click on the **Share & save** button, and hit **Done**.

If a collaborator is working on the same spreadsheet, at the same time we are, we can see it below the **Comments** and **Share** buttons as shown in the following screenshot:

If we click on the arrow next to **1 other viewer**, we can chat directly with the collaborator as we edit it collaboratively:

Remember that, this can be quite useful in distance courses that have collaborative tasks assigned to groups.

Creating a shared folder using Google Drive

We can also use the sharing functionality to share documents with the collaborators (15 GB of space for that). In the main Google Drive page, we can create a folder by navigating to **Create | Folder**. We are then required to give it a name:

The folder will be shown in the files and folder explorer in Google Drive:

To share it with someone, we need to right-click the folder and choose the **Share...** option. Then, just like the process of sharing a spreadsheet we saw previously, we just need to add our collaborators' contacts (for example, e-mail) in the **Invite people:** field, then click on **Share & save**, and hit **Done**. The invited people will receive an e-mail to add the shared folder to their Google Drive (they need a Google account for this) and it is done. Everything we add to this folder is automatically synced with everyone. This includes all the Google Drive documents, PDFs, and all the files uploaded to this folder. And it's an easy way to share multimedia projects between a group of people working on the same project.

Creating floor plans using Floorplanner

Designing spaces can be an interesting activity in several subjects, starting at the conceptual stage with digital prototyping, and including trial of solutions, without a great deal of effort. We could use a Floorplanner to design:

- A new school laboratory
- A photography studio
- The school we want
- A yard
- An eco-friendly house
- An activity for language teaching, where students have to name objects in different spaces
- A set for a drama performance
- A setting in which characters of a book move around, as a support for creative writing

In the good old days, when computers were rare, I built a music studio with an old friend of mine. At that time, we had neither the money nor the fancy digital floor planners, so we just used the usual techniques of buying cheap stuff, and trial and error, moving instruments and equipments repeatedly until we found the perfect configuration. We got egg boxes from a friend who had a cake factory, some old carpets from a neighbor, cork and Styrofoam for the doors, walls, and ceiling, and an old hatch to make a window in a previously-scary, dark, and humid basement. We were thrilled with the result—a decent studio from little money. I remember we called it Studio 2, as at that time I had a 1990 Mini of that model. That's where I got the idea for the following course activity.

In *Module 6, Spaces for music,* following the budgeting of the studio, we saw previously with Google Drive, students are asked to create a 3D representation of the studio of their dreams by using an online Floorplanner tool.

Floorplanner (`http://www.floorplanner.com`) is an online planning tool that allows us to create one floor plan for free, which can be seen in 3D and embedded anywhere, including, in our Moodle courses.

After signing up and logging in, we are taken to **Dashboard**, where we can manage our account and create our first project by clicking on **Create new project**, as shown in the following screenshot.

We can then start entering the details for the floor plan, and, when done, hit the **Create Project** button as shown in the following screenshot:

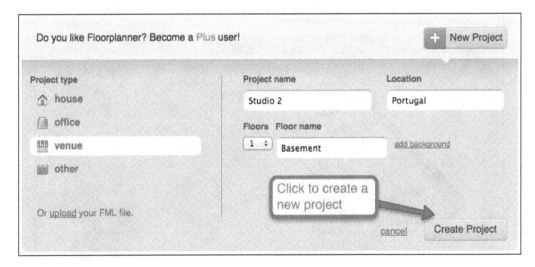

Creating a room

We are then presented with the workspace, with a sidebar on the left and a drawing interface on the right:

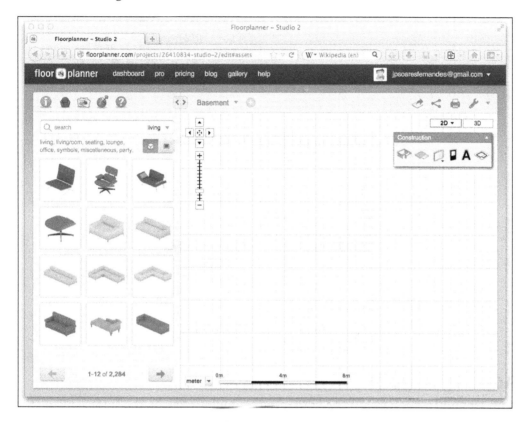

The steps is to create our music studio are:

1. Click on the draw room icon in the **Construction** toolbar present at the upper-right corner. The mouse pointer changes to a black cross.

2. Click on the squared area, and drag the mouse to make a rectangle of the size that you want for your studio.

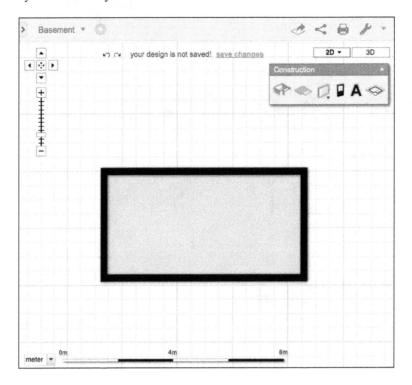

Adding a floor

Now, let's add a floor to our room. We need to double-click on the surface inside the room that we've just created, and then select one of the patterns for the floor of our room from the pop-up window:

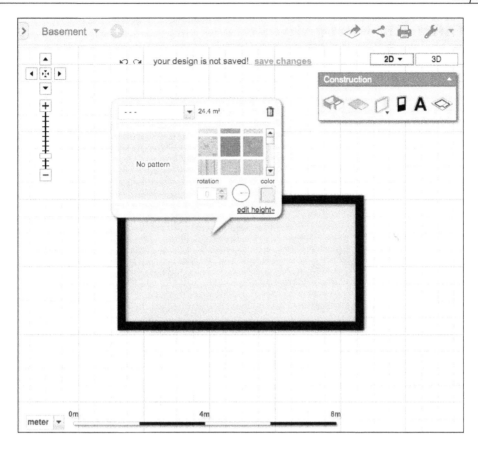

Adding construction elements

We can now add doors, windows, and walls to the plan. For example, if we click on the door icon in the **Construction** toolbar, we will get a library of elements that we can drag onto the plan, such as doors and windows.

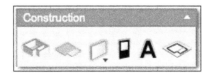

Adding furniture elements

To add furniture and other elements to the studio, we should use the search field in the sidebar, and enter the required furniture name.

We can then drag the elements to the plan and position them where we want them.

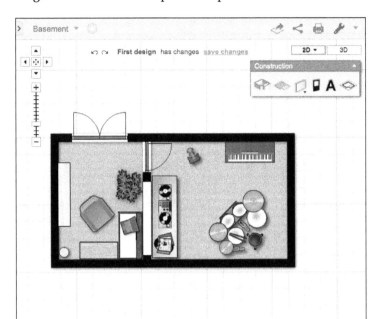

We can rotate the elements, move them around, and if we click on the furniture, we can also change its properties, duplicate, or delete them.

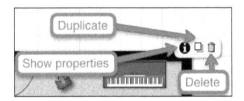

Saving and publishing

We have to make sure that we save our design before leaving the Floorplanner, by using the **save changes** notice located on top of the drawing area.

If we click on the **3D** button above the **Construction** toolbar, we can see a three-dimensional view of the plan.

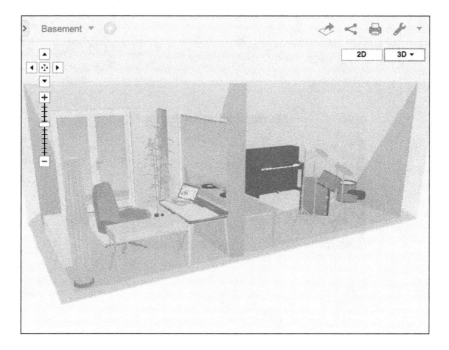

Once we're done, we have at least two options to add our floor plan to Moodle:

- Export as image
- Embed

Export as image

In the menu at the upper-right corner, above the **Construction** toolbar, the first button on the left allows us to export the plan as an image:

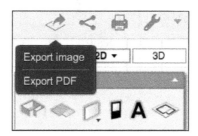

On a free account, the only image size allowed is 640 × 480 px. We can later upload this file to Moodle, as we saw in *Chapter 2*, *Picture This*.

Embed

If we want to embed or link to it from within Moodle, we should go to the upper-right corner of the web page, and click on **My account**.

In the left menu, after clicking on the **Projects** item, there's a button **Actions** next to our project.

We can get the embed code provided, and add it to our course.

Creating mind maps using Mindomo

Mind maps are an excellent technique for students to perform connections among concepts and to help them think about subjects. They can be used as a nice revision tool as well. In our course, one of the activities in *Module 4, Music as a language*, deals with creating a mind map about some of the music theory concepts. We will use a tool called Mindomo to create this mind map.

Mindomo (`http://www.mindomo.com`) is an online mind map software that we can use to create multimedia mind maps with text, videos, images, and hyperlinks.

With a basic free account, we can create three mind maps. After signing up, we can create a new mind map by clicking on the **Create** button on the dashboard.

We are then required to fill in some details about the map and when done, hit the **Ok** button.

Adding topics

The most important functions for a start are, to add topic and subtopic (present on the top toolbar), and add multimedia elements to the topics (present on the left toolbar).

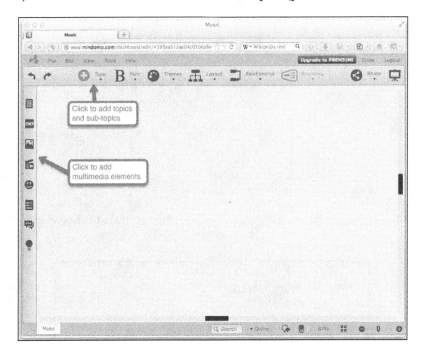

For now, let's start by giving the main topic the name Music, and add some more subtopics by clicking on the **Topic** option and then on **Subtopic**:

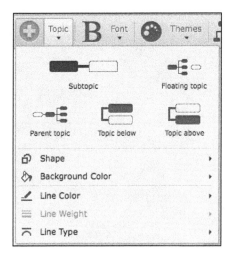

We will get something like this:

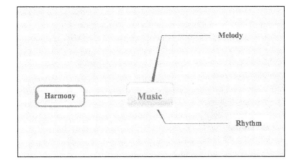

Adding multimedia elements

To add videos, images, or hyperlinks, follow these steps:

1. Click on one of the topics or subtopics in the workspace.
2. Click on the required icon on the left toolbar.
3. In the pop-up box, fill in the details and click on the **Set** button.

As an example, let's see how to add a YouTube video to the Harmony subtopic.

After clicking on the Add Multimedia button in the left toolbar, we can search for videos on YouTube (or Vimeo) or directly add the URL of the video:

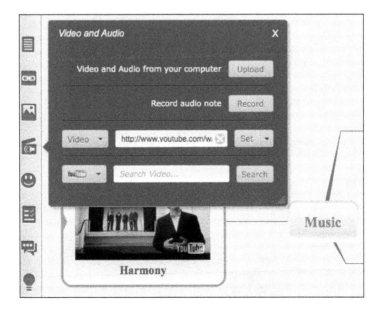

We will get something similar to the following screenshot, with videos showing up inside the subtopic:

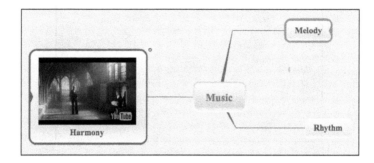

Besides videos, we can record audio notes, upload videos, add hyperlinks or images.

Saving and publishing

Finally, we can save the mind map by clicking on the **Save** option under the **File** menu item found in the upper-left corner. To get the URL or embed code for Moodle integration, so that we can share the mind map, there is a **Share** button in the upper-right corner. If we click on this button, and then on **Embed in website**, the embed code will be copied to the clipboard, and we can then paste it in Moodle.

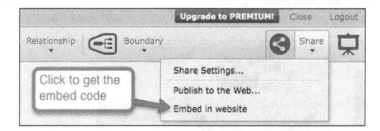

Creating interactive timelines using Tiki-Toki

Interactive timelines can be very useful for illustrating historical events and change through time, allowing us to have a better visual perspective on the succession of events that lead to a particular moment. From major events in your life to the history of a game, a country, a theory, a person, or a sequence of news items that came out about a subject, many uses can be thought of for this kind of tool. Now imagine adding images, audio, video, and hyperlinks to it, along with some nice navigation, and you'll realize the added value of this tool.

In our course, in *Module 1*, *Music evolves*, one of the activities will require students to create timelines of particular music genres selected by them, and include audio, video, and hyperlinked references related to this genre.

Tiki-Toki (`http://www.tiki-toki.com`) is an online tool that allows us to create interactive multimedia timelines. It requires registration, and is free to use, so every student can create his or her own account.

After signing up, we have to create a timeline by filling up some information about it, and click on the **Create new timeline** button, as shown in the following screenshot:

Adding a story

After creating the timeline, the first step is to create a new story. To do this, perform the following steps:

1. Click on the **ADMIN** item in the top-right corner.

2. Click on **CREATE NEW STORY**.

3. Fill the information in the **Basic Info** tab (**Title**, **Start date**, **End date**, **Intro**, and **Link**):

Adding multimedia

We can now add multimedia content to our story by clicking on the **Story media** tab, and then clicking on **ADD NEW MEDIA**.

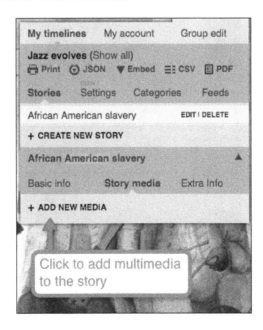

We can then add a link to an image, video, or audio. Let's try a video.

After we click on the **Save** button, the timeline will show a new story with the picture that we have selected as thumb:

And if we click on the **More** button, we can read all the information and watch the video, as shown in the following screenshot:

Sharing

After adding all of the events to the timeline, we can get the link to the timeline on our browser and share it in our Moodle course. Unfortunately, the embed code is disabled for free accounts, (and group editing as well).

Creating dynamic maps using Google Maps Engine

Accessing images from all around the world was impossible some years ago. We are talking about huge amounts of information in photos taken by satellites, or produced by geographers and earth scientists. Such information wasn't available to everyone in a practical way.

We will require students to create an online map in *Module 2*, *A world of music*, to illustrate the geographical history of some instruments from around the world. Some of these instruments, such as the ukulele, travelled thousands of kilometers—it was taken by Portuguese sailors to Hawaii.

Google Maps Engine (`https://mapsengine.google.com`) is one of several online map services available, that allow us to search and navigate in this sea of geographical information.

Besides that, it also makes available various tools that make these maps more interesting for teaching and learning. These tools are markers, lines, and shapes; these are the digital equivalents of the elements we would use in real, paper-based maps, to represent information about them. The advantage here is the possibilities that multimedia brings. For example, we can use this in activities to:

- Display places of interest with multimedia placemarks (earthquakes, volcanoes, schools, animals from several biomes, historical buildings, events such as battles, and so on)

- Draw lines and areas on the maps (illustrating routes or regions, for example, the trip of a Portuguese navigator Vasco da Gama from Portugal to India, administrative regions, or the plan of a study visit to a nature reserve)

Creating a new map

After we log in to our Google account, we just need to go back to Google Maps Engine and click on the **New map** button.

We will now need to complete a form, giving the title of the map and a description, and hitting the **Save** button:

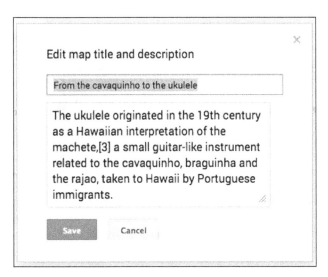

Adding a marker

Adding a marker is very simple. The first thing to do is to find a place where we want to put it. For this, we have two options:

- Drag the map in any direction with the mouse (keeping the map clicked), and use the scroll wheel to zoom in or zoom out, or just use the navigation interface to the left of the map.

- Search for a place in the search field. Google Maps Engine will add a green marker to the destination. Click on it and then on the **Add to map** link.

Google Maps Engine has several types of maps that we can display—road maps, satellite imagery, terrain information, and in some cases, street views and traffic information as well. To select the appropriate one, we should select a base map from the left menu, as shown in the following image:

Now, let's take a look at the marker. There's a toolbar for adding elements to the map, on the upper-left corner of the map region.

We should click on the Add marker button on the toolbar, next to the hand tool, and position it where we want to add the marker to the map.

Now, in the provided pop up, we can insert all of the information that we want to include, in the title and description fields.

Adding a line

To suggest a connection between placemarks (for example, a route), we can add lines to our map, connecting the placemarks. After clicking on the Add line or shape icon in the toolbar, we just click on the starting point. Next, we can click on as many additional points as we wish. In this way, a line will be drawn between the points that we select. When we are done, we just need to double-click at that location.

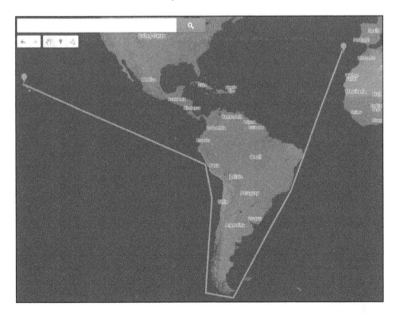

Sharing and collaborating

In the upper-right corner of our map, we can see a **Share** button:

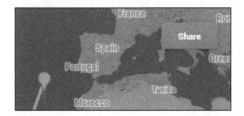

If we click on this, we can add collaborators like we have seen in Google Drive.

To embed the map in Moodle, we first have to change its privacy settings.

We should select the **Public on the web** under **Visibility options:** and hit **Save** and then click on **Done**.

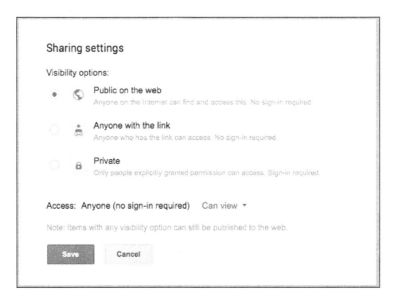

Now, to get the embed code, we should click on the folder icon on the left and then click on the **Embed on my site** option.

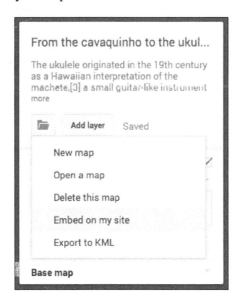

Just a quick reference of Google Earth (http://earth.google.com) to finish this section on online maps. This is a computer software application that uses the same map data as Google Maps. It has more functionality than the latter (you can work in 3D, explore the Moon, Mars, and sky maps, insert GPS data, and take measurements).

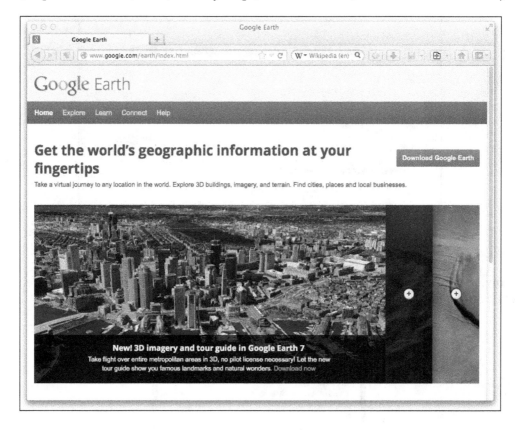

Creating a dynamic presentation using Prezi

Online presentations are a great way of providing students with the opportunity to develop their presentation skills. And I'm not just talking about creating PowerPoint-like presentations, but of presenting and discussing by using audio and video. Some uses for this can be:

- Create online presentations or discussions around slideshows, screenshots, pictures, music, or video (of a study trip, works of art, an idea, a political cartoon, an experiment, football game tactics, a trainee teacher's class, and so on)
- Introduce students to each other by showing some of their photos, work, and/or videos (or to critique their own work)

The advantage of this kind of presentation is that we don't need to be at the same place at the same time to make this happen. Another advantage is that, using Moodle alone for this doesn't provide the same kind of flexibility and speed of use (we would have to use a forum, do a lot of uploads of multimedia elements, and all of this multiplied by the number of students).

In our course, the context for using this tool will be a final course event, where every student will have to present their best works in 20 slides, with only 20 seconds to spend talking about each (their colleagues will have to comment on them, too). This presentation format is called Pecha Kucha, and started in the young designers' world as a way of showing their works in an efficient way. The 20 x 20 format allows a total presentation time of 6 minutes 40 seconds per person, which is enough time to show important stuff.

Prezi (`http://prezi.com`) is a presentation tool that allows us to produce interactive presentations in an easy way.

After we sign up for a free account, we have 100 MB of storage to create our Prezi presentations. To start a new one, we just have to click on the **New prezi** button on the dashboard.

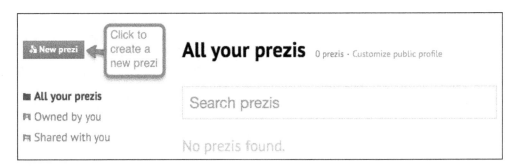

We will then be required to select a template for our presentation. We should select it and hit the **Use template** button.

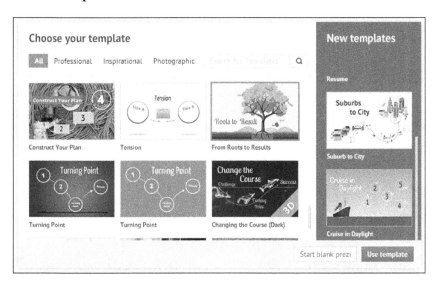

We are then presented with an editing window, with a panel on the left, with several path points (what we call slides). Remember that, Prezi is an interactive presentation that moves around a path using transitions between slides, in a dynamic way.

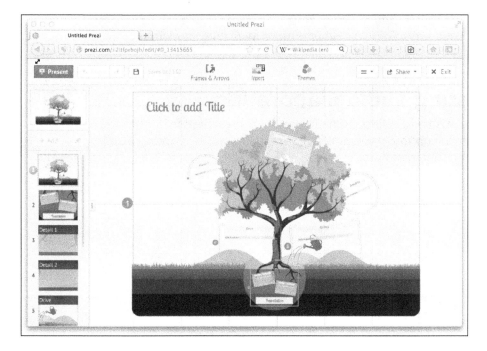

In the provided template, there's a path already built-in, to which we can add our own content. In the first slide, we can add a title by clicking on the **Click to add Title** text.

In the second slide, for example, we can add our title, and insert a YouTube video, using the **Insert** option in the top menu:

Using the option **Add Voice-over to Path Step #2.**, we can narrate our Prezi presentation too. There are other options available, that we can use according to the type of assignment we want to show our audience (PDF, Image, Diagram, and so on.)

Sharing and collaborating

We can also add collaborators to our Prezi presentation. Under the **Share** button, the option **Share prezi...** allows us to add by e-mail, people who can also edit the presentation.

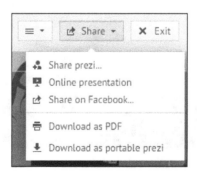

To make an online presentation, where our audience sees in real time, slide by slide, what we are showing as a presenter, we should first save the Prezi, and hit the **Exit** button.

We are then taken to the presentation page, and we should hit the **Present online** button.

We are then presented with a link we should post in Moodle, and we wait for the audience to show up.

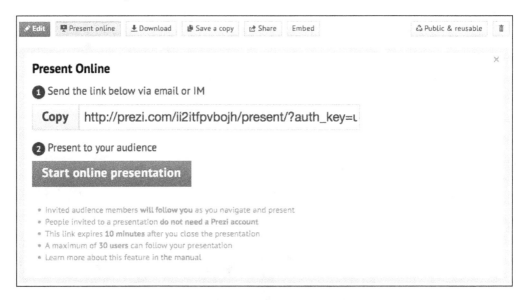

Also, notice the **Embed** button at the top. We can use the provided code to embed our Prezi presentation in Moodle.

Summary

In this chapter, we focused on activities we can perform by using Moodle and some web-based applications. The objective was to show how this integration can open several possibilities for teaching and learning, providing free applications where teachers and students can create their own multimedia works, and then embed them in Moodle for instruction, discussion, or assessment. We created interactive charts, floor plans, timelines, maps, and online presentations, to represent data and mind maps. We also saw the possibilities of having collaboration in the construction of these multimedia works, as most web applications have a standard option to create a collective work with others. But to achieve this, we need assessment tools to complement the ones provided by Moodle. In the next chapter, we will learn how to add multimedia to Moodle quizzes and lessons, create interactive exercises, and assess multimedia works with rubrics.

6
Multimedia and Assessments

In this chapter, we will create assessment activities using multimedia. We will use images, audio, and video to create interactive exercises, either by using Moodle's quizzes, lessons, or assignments, or by using external tools such as Hot Potatoes and JClic, which can later be integrated into our course.

By the end of this chapter you will be:

- Adding multimedia to multiple choice answers in Moodle quizzes and lessons
- Creating crosswords and jumble exercises in Hot Potatoes
- Creating puzzles and find-the-pair activities using JClic
- Assessing multimedia work using rubrics
- Integrating all of these activities into Moodle

Adding multimedia to multiple choice answers in Moodle quizzes and lessons

Sometimes it can be useful to insert multimedia elements into the answers of a multiple choice question in a Moodle lesson or quiz. This can apply to situations where students are required to:

- Recognize audio excerpts corresponding to text, images, or videos (for example, in music or language courses students have to identify a melody from a music sheet excerpt, or the correct pronunciation of a given text)
- Recognize video scenes (for example, corresponding to a certain dialogue, and gestural conversation)

Adding multimedia to the question body is fairly easy because we can use the text editor and just link to a multimedia file, and the Moodle filter will do the rest. But adding questions for which the answer choices are multimedia files is a different story, as there is no text editor in lessons, just a simple text form. However, this is not complicated with the help of a correct HTML code.

For example, in the course, *Module 1, Music evolves*, students have to post excerpts of songs from different moments of a musical genre to a forum topic as attachments (see *Chapter 3, Sound and Music*, for details on slicing audio). In the same module, we will create a quiz (*Mini-quiz – history of music*) that will use the excerpts posted by our students in its questions, as an incentive for other students to have a look at their colleagues' work.

So, after creating a new quiz and adding a new multiple choice question to it (for example, "Which of the following excerpts refers to a medieval music?") we can add links to the MP3 files submitted by students as choices (or to the files in our course files area). We can get these links as we saw previously, by right-clicking (*control + click for Mac users*) on the linked MP3 file in the forum post, and then clicking on the **Copy Link Location** option, as shown in the following screenshot:

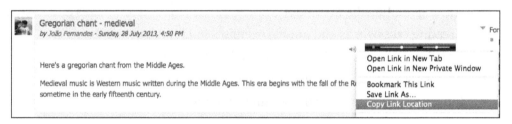

Next, while editing the multiple choice question, we can add a link to the link location in the answer form. This is an easy way, as Moodle, with its multimedia filter, will do the rest:

As a result, we'll get something like this:

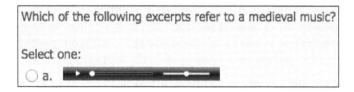

The same concept applies for videos and music from online services such as YouTube, as we can paste the embed code in the answer form. Add the embed code in the following manner:

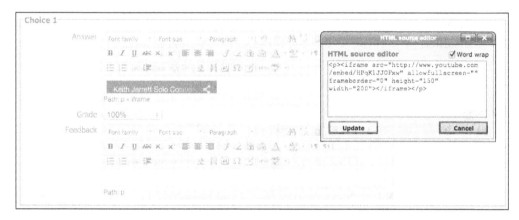

On adding the embed code, the question will look like the following screenshot:

When using this process, we should keep a few things in mind:

- The multimedia files that are linked in the choice options must be available to the students in the course. If we copy the link location from the files area but the file itself is not available to the students, we'll have problems. The same applies to attachments in forum posts with separate groups.

- Consider a situation where the files linked to in the answer options are those of an attachment in a forum post on the course. Suppose, the question is shared and the quiz is restored in another course or exported to another Moodle installation. In this case, there will be problems with the file access, as the hyperlink will point to the original source in a particular course, which is not currently available.

- In the case of video or audio from online services, embedding may be disabled by request, so these can become unavailable later in the course.

- Too many links to MP3 files on the same quiz page, and/or MP3 files of considerable size can slow down the page loading.

As a possible solution to the first three issues, we can have the multimedia files in a public folder on our server. In this way, files can be accessed from different courses and domains. We could, for example, download a YouTube video and make it available on our server, if this service is blocked in our school or institution (see *Chapter 4*, *Video*, for information on this). Another option is to upload these files to the course files area (but in this case, the files must be made available to students in the course, or they will not have permission to listen or view them).

As a possible solution to the last issue, we can use page breaks, or have one question per page in the quiz, so that students can only load one question at a time. Another solution is to reduce the size of the files, either by slicing or by encoding the files in other formats. In the case of an MP3, reducing the bitrate could be an option (see *Chapter 3*, *Sound and Music* for information on this).

Adding multimedia to quizzes, lessons, and assignments

Remember that, multimedia can be used in interesting ways not only in multiple choice answers, but also in question bodies, lesson content, and assignments. We can create lessons in a tutorial style, with videos, followed by questions on the video's content, leading to different lesson branches according to the answers, or assignments can be presented as quick briefing videos. And don't forget that if we want to receive multimedia assignments, we should set this activity to allow students' file uploads.

Creating exercises with Hot Potatoes

Hot Potatoes (`http://hotpot.uvic.ca`) from Half-Baked Software allow us to create interactive web games and puzzles in a simple way. One of the advantages of Hot Potatoes over Moodle's quiz engine is that, Hot Potatoes makes it easier to create exercises, and some of these are very different from the ones available in Moodle, for example crosswords, and finding pairs via drag-and-drop. We can download the software from `http://hotpot.uvic.ca/index.php#downloads`.

There are six different types of exercises that we can create with this software:

- **JQuiz**: They are question-based exercises
- **JCloze**: They are fill in the gaps exercises
- **JMatch**: They are matching exercises
- **JMix**: They are jumble exercises
- **JCross**: They are crosswords
- **The Masher**: They are the linked exercises of the different types mentioned above

We will only take a look at the **JCross** and **JMix** exercises, as the other formats can be achieved with the question types that Moodle provides in quizzes and lessons. However, you should try them and see for yourself how easy it can be!

JCross – Crosswords

In our course, *Module 4, Music as a language,* students have to deal with a lot of new concepts on basic music theory. A crossword exercise can be a good way to recall some of these.

After opening Hot Potatoes and clicking on the **JCross** potato, we see the standard interface, a grid, in which we can start creating a crossword exercise. We can start by adding a title to the exercise on the leftmost pane, labeled **Title**.

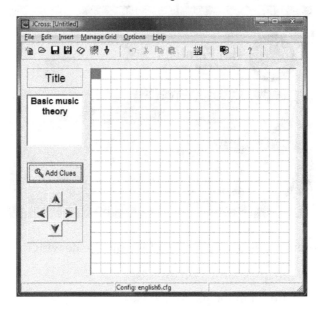

Then, we can click on the third button from the right on the toolbar, to create a grid layout automatically, from a list of words that we provide.

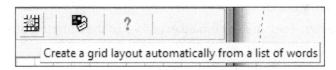

We can then enter each word or phrase on a separate line, similar to the following example, and then click on the **Make the grid** button. We can also define the maximum grid size, in this case the default of 20 × 20 letters. When we export the exercise as HTML to include it in Moodle, this will automatically be adjusted to the size of the words in the exercise.

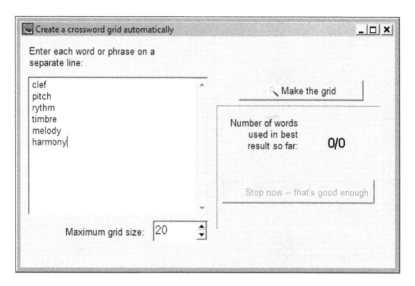

When the grid is ready, we would get something like this:

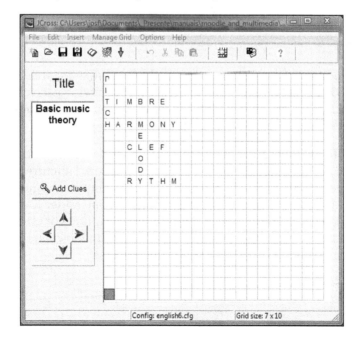

Next, we need to define the clues, just like in any crossword exercise, by clicking on the button **Add Clues**, below the title. We will then get a list of the words in our crosswords exercise.

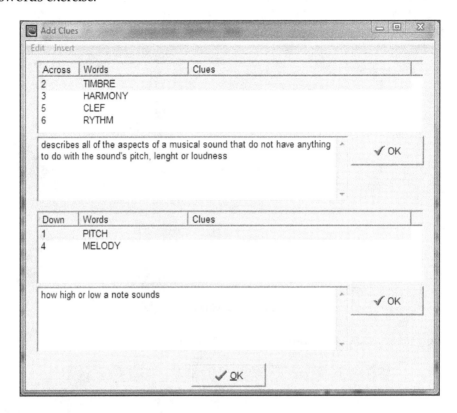

Here, we just need to click on each word and add the clue in the field provided, clicking on the **OK** button adjacent to the field after specifying each clue. We can also add pictures, URLs, or other media (videos and Flash) to the clues by using the **Insert** menu. Let's look at how to add an image.

For the word **CLEF**, we could insert a picture of a bass clef, so that students can see a clue for the word. To do this, we need to navigate to **Insert | Picture | Picture from Local File** and then select an image of a clef from our computer. Again, remember that we need to always keep files for a single project in one folder to avoid images disappearing when the exercise is used on different computers or on the Web. We should first save the Hot Potatoes project in a folder, and then create an images folder where we can put all of the images for this exercise.

So, after selecting a picture of a bass clef from our images folder, we would get the following configuration window:

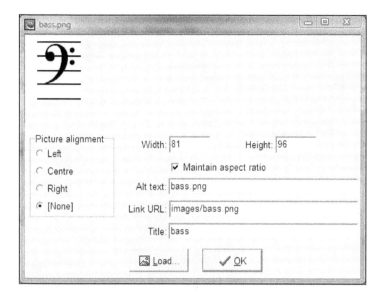

After we click on the **OK** button, our crossword exercise is ready, with the HTML code for the image already inserted.

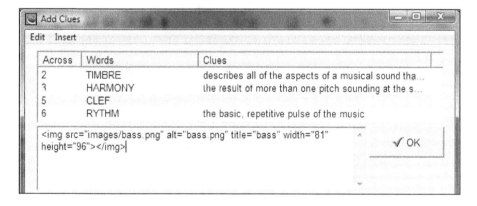

We just need to export it by pressing the *F6* key or by clicking on the button to the left of the downwards red arrow on the toolbar. We can then save it in our project folder, and preview it in the browser.

JMix – Jumble exercises

With JMix we can create jumbled phrases or words, and students will have to put the jumbled parts into the correct order. In our course, *Module 5, Being a musician,* students have to write about their favorite artists. We can build on this by creating a JMix exercise (or by letting students create one) that works as a review for some of the facts that they identified about these artists (again, this is an incentive for the colleagues to read what others have done).

After clicking on the **JMix** potato, we can start by adding a title and saving our JMix file.

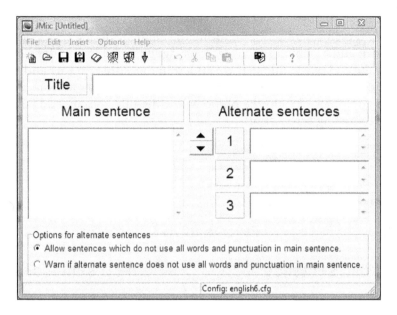

Then, in the **Main sentence** form, we can insert a sentence separated by breaks. For example, to break up the sentence "Richard Bona was born in the Cameroon in 1967" into word segments, you would type this into the **Main sentence** box as shown in the following screenshot:

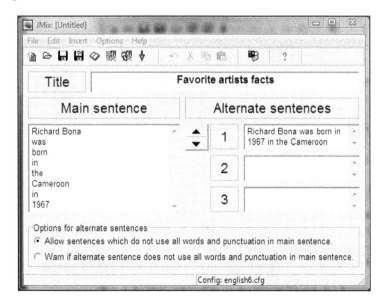

Note that, in this case the phrase could be written in two ways, so there was the need to add an alternative sentence so that students can provide either answer and still be marked correct.

We can also add pictures and other multimedia elements to the title. For example, in this case we can add a photo of Richard Bona, again stored in a folder called `images`. Next, click at the end of the title that we added in the **Title** window and then go to **Insert | Picture | Picture from Local File** and select the photo from the `images` folder on our computer. To add the photo below the title, we can add a break tag, as shown in the following screenshot:

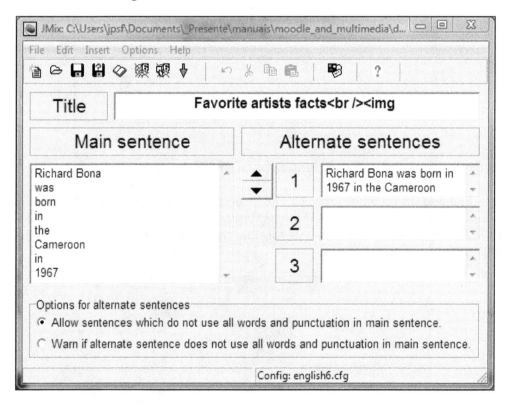

Publish

Finally, we need to export the exercise as HTML. For this type of exercise, we can export in two formats — with the drag-and-drop functionality (*Ctrl + F6*) or without the drag-and-drop functionality (*F6*). We can also use the export buttons on the toolbar. As an example, here's the screenshot of an exercise with drag-and-drop functionality:

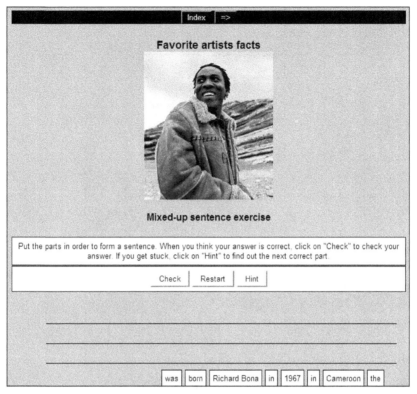

Richard Bona's picture source: RV's agen (2006). Richard Bona 1.jpg. Retrieved October 10, 2008, from http://en.wikipedia.org/wiki/File:Richard_Bona-1.jpg

Moodle it!

Hot Potatoes produces an HTML file that we can add as an activity in Moodle 2.5 if we have the plugin installed. We just need to upload the HTML file together with the images and other elements that we used in the exercise (for example, Richard Bona's picture) to our course files area, and then point to the HTML file from the Hot Potatoes activity settings. Let's try it with the JCross exercise that we just created. We should upload the HTML file generated by the Hot Potatoes software, along with all of the multimedia files that we attached (in this case, an images folder and its contents).

We can, for example, send a ZIP file of the HTML and the folder, and later unzip it in Moodle.

This resource should point to the `.htm` file.

We will get a result similar to the following screenshot:

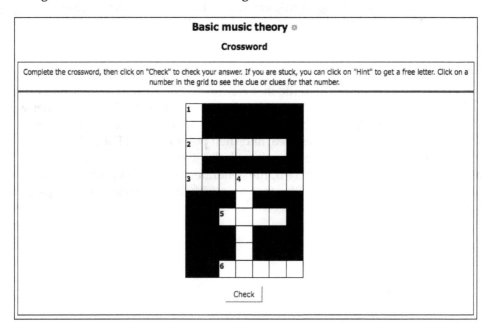

One of the advantages of integrating Hot Potatoes in this way, rather than just as a resource, has to do with Moodle keeping logs of students' activity in the exercise, which can be of help if we want to see what they've been doing. Another advantage is the easy way of creating quizzes, when compared to Moodle's quiz engine.

Creating interactive exercises with JClic

JClic (`http://clic.xtec.net/en`) is a free (under the GPL license, more about this in *Chapter 8, Common Multimedia Issues in Moodle*) software application released by the Ministry of Education of the Government of Catalunya. It is written in Java, and allows us to create the following seven types of interactive activities:

- **Association games**: They are used to identify the relationship between two groups of data

- **Memory games**: They are used to discover hidden pairs of elements

- **Exploring, Identifying, and Information games**: They start with initial information, and the user has to choose paths to the answer

- **Puzzles**: They are used to order graphics, text, and audio, or to combine graphics and audio

- **Written answers**: They are used to write text, a word, or a sentence

- **Text activities**: They are used to solve exercises based on words, sentences, letters, and paragraphs (these can be completed, corrected, or ordered)

- **Word searches and crosswords**: They are used to find hidden words or solve crossword puzzles

JClic exercises can be more visually appealing than Hot Potatoes, as we will see, and can be particularly useful for younger students. But, as they require Java, this should be checked with the ICT coordinator as Java must be installed on the schools' PCs.

In the software download area (`http://clic.xtec.cat/en/jclic/download.htm`), we can download **JClic author**, the application that allows us to create these activities. The file will use WebStart, and will run from a single file, named `jclic.jnlp`. When we run it for the first time, in Microsoft Vista at least, we will need to give permission for the application to run (selecting the **Always trust content from this publisher** option will avoid having to perform this step every time we start JClic):

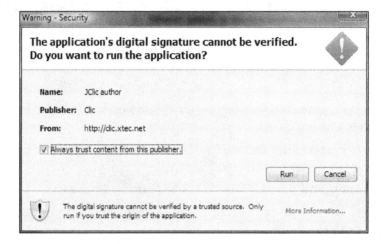

Then JClic will start loading:

The interface of JClic author is as shown in the following screenshot:

As it can be seen, there are four available tabs:

- **Project**: It is the default tab, which allows us to define some details of the project.
- **Media library**: It is where pictures and other multimedia are managed.
- **Activities**: It is where the project activities are created or modified. This tab further contains four tabs.
- **Sequences**: where we can sequence several activities in the same project.

The options inside these tabs will be available only after we create a new project.

Starting a new project

The first step in building interactive JClic activities is to start a new project (by navigating to **File | New project**).

We should then define:

- The name of the project
- The name of the file in which the project will be saved (having a double extension of .jclic.zip)
- The default folder for saving the files

  The name of the default folder is same as the name of your project, and is located at the following location:

  - ° C:/Programme Files/JClic/projects (in Windows)
  - ° $home/JClic/projects (in other OS)

We can change the default folder location, and if we are using multimedia files, we should keep everything organized inside that folder.

Creating a puzzle activity

We are now ready to start creating our first activity, a puzzle. In *Module 2, A world of music*, we can pick some of the pictures of instruments that our students gathered in the Instrument Mappers activities and create a jigsaw puzzle as part of a final game for the module. We will perform the following steps:

1. Provide the details of the project in the **Project** tab.
2. Import a picture in the **Media library** tab.
3. Add an activity called Exchangeable puzzle.
4. Create a sequence.

Note that, we are starting from the tab on the left and moving to the right as we configure the activity.

As an example, I created a project called `Instruments`:

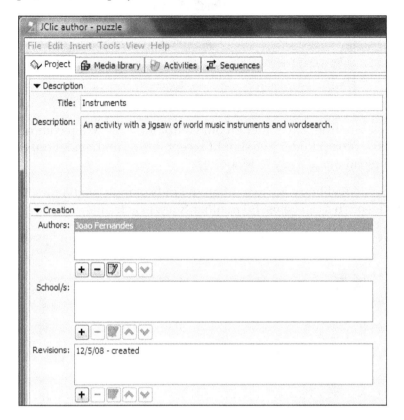

Next, I added a description of the activity and specified myself as an author by clicking on the **+** button. We can specify more details, but for now this much information is enough as an example.

Now, let's import a picture in the **Media library** tab by clicking on the icon on the far left on the toolbar:

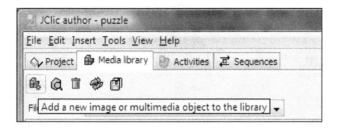

If we pick a picture from any folder on our computer, JClic will recommend that this be copied to the project folder (we should accept this recommendation, especially if we want to upload our activity to Moodle).

Note that, the Media library accepts different kinds of multimedia files, from MP3 to Flash, and Video. This can be useful in other types of activities.

We now have a picture of a **lamelaphone** that will make a difficult jigsaw for our students.

Lamelaphone image source: Weeks, Alex (2006). Mbira dzavadzimu 1.jpg. Retrieved October 12, 2008, from
`http://commons.wikimedia.org/wiki/File:Mbira_dzavadzimu_1.jpg`

The next step is to add the puzzle activity, in the **Activities** tab, by clicking on the icon on the far left of the toolbar.

A dialog box is displayed, and in this menu we should select the **Exchange puzzle** option and enter a name for our puzzle in the input field at the bottom of the dialog box.

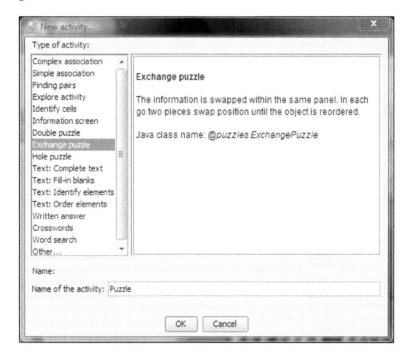

We can then add a description for the activity, and if needed we can define a timer countdown (in the **Counters** section), among other options.

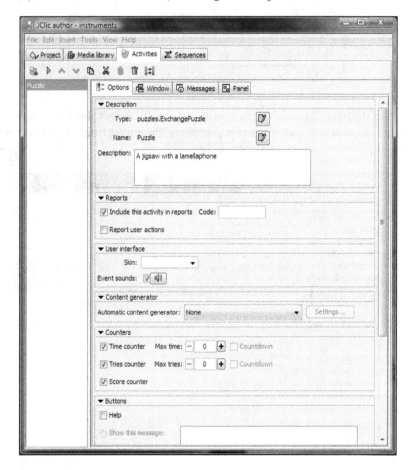

 Reports are also mentioned in this dialog box. Using this, JClic provides a way to gather students' responses. But due to the complexity of this functionality, we will not deal with it in this book.

In the **Window** tab under the the **Activities** tab, we can also define some color options, as shown in the following screenshot:

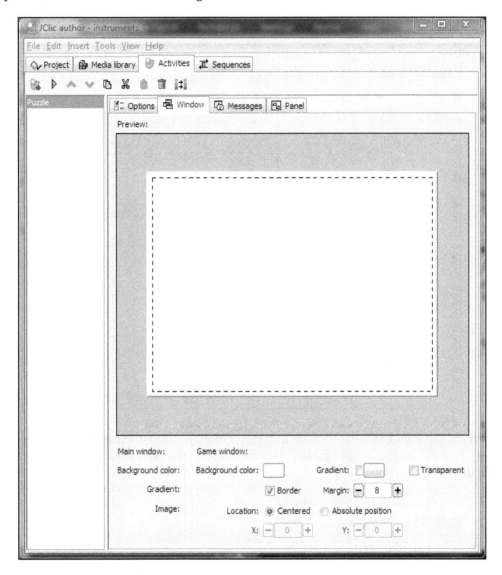

In the **Messages** tab, we can add an initial message, which for example, gives the context of the activity, and a final message as feedback for the exercise, by clicking on the dark gray areas.

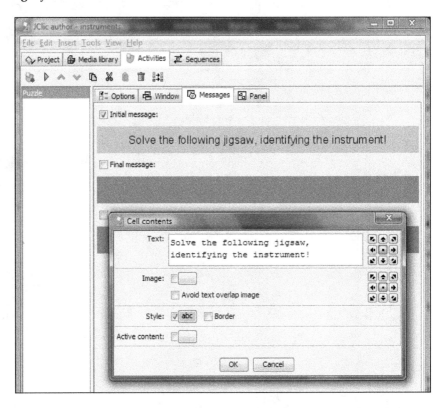

Finally, in the **Panel** tab, we should insert the lamelaphone's picture from our Media library and define the kind of jigsaw that we want. In the next screenshot, I have done the following three things:

1. Selected a jigsaw with curved unions.
2. Defined 5 × 5 pieces.
3. Selected an image from the Media library.

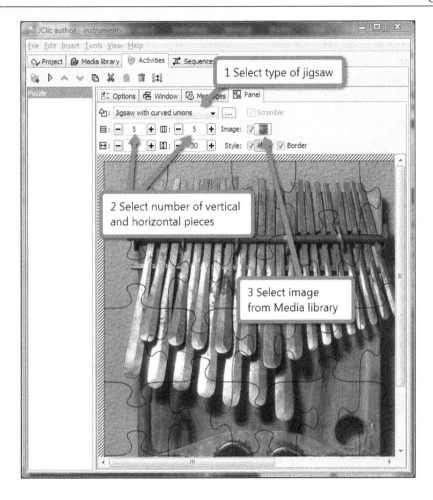

Our puzzle activity is now ready, and we can now add a finding pairs activity to the same project, in a sequence.

Creating a finding pairs activity

Finding pairs activities (where students have to locate pairs of similar pictures or in ear training exercises) can be interesting for memory exercises, and in our course in particular. In this example, students have to pick pairs of sounds with the same note from different world instruments.

After adding a new finding pairs activity (using the same process that we saw previously for the puzzle), we should add MP3 files of the instrument sounds to our Media library. After this, in the **Panel** tab we can define the size of the grid (in this case a 3 x 3 grid) and then start associating the MP3 files to each cell in the grid. To do this, carry out the following steps:

1. Click on one of the cells of the grid.

2. In the pop-up window, click on the **Active content** button (similarly, if we wanted to add images, we would use the **Image** button instead).

3. In the pop-up window, click on the **Play sound** button and then select the sound file from the Media library.

4. Click on the **OK** button.

5. In the textbox, add the letter of the note, just as a reference that this cell has been populated (we will delete this reference in step 7. We need to do this because we are dealing with sounds in this edit mode. With images or text it would be easier as we would have a visual reference).

6. Click on the **OK** button.

7. Remove the reference text in the textboxes for all of the rectangles.

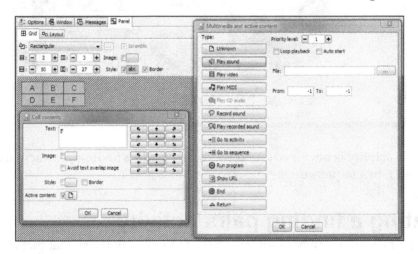

Now, in the **Layout** tab, choose the position of the pair of this grid (the one that we edited is grid A; this can appear on the left, right, top, or bottom of the automatically created grid B). Students will have to connect an element on one grid with the similar element on the other grid.

Sequencing activities

Finally, we will need to sequence the activities that we have just created. In the **Sequences** tab, if we click on the play button, we will see a preview of the selected activity. The activity will be added automatically to the sequence list.

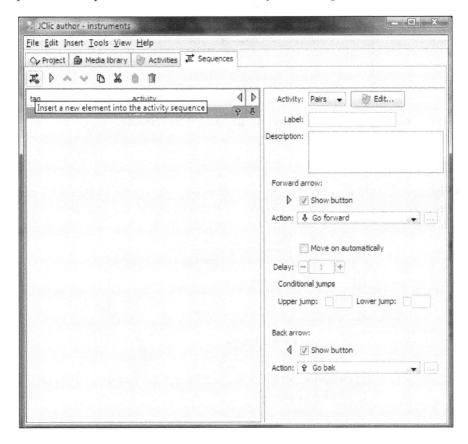

Note that, we can either show or hide the navigation buttons in our sequence by using the options in the right-hand pane.

We can add more activities to the sequence by clicking on the button on the far left of the toolbar.

We are now ready to publish the project and add it to Moodle.

Publish

To publish the activity as a Web page, we just need to navigate to **Tools** | **Create web page....** In the configuration window that is displayed, we just need to click on **OK** and then **Save**.

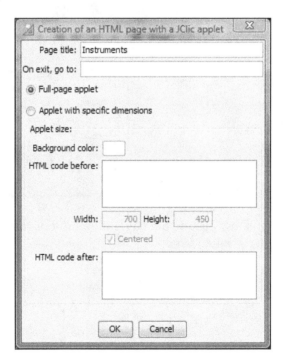

As a result, we will have an `index.htm` file and a `.jclic.zip` file, both ready to be uploaded to Moodle.

Moodle it!

In Moodle, we can now add a resource, which is a link to a file or website, and upload both the files, `index.htm` and `instruments.jclic.zip` to the course files (we don't need to upload these files to the same folder). This resource should point to the `index.htm` file.

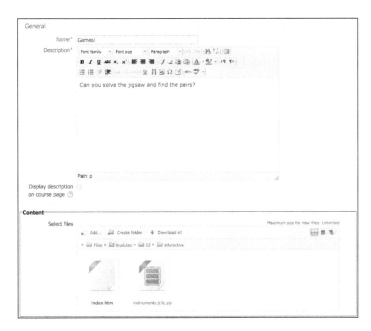

And the final result is as shown in the following screenshot:

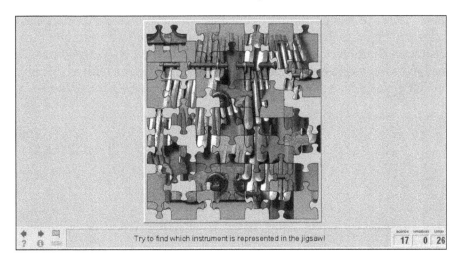

We can also design an activity where a group of students can create games like these for each other.

Assessing multimedia using rubrics

A rubric is a scoring tool that lists the criteria by which a work will be assessed, along with the several levels of achievement for these criteria. In some countries this can be defined by an exam board, while in others, it's left to the school to decide. In either case, this is a great way of providing students with the assessment criteria in which they are expected to achieve, in advance, and make the work of teachers easier, as the scoring is very quick. A rubric could look something like the following:

Criteria/ Level	1	2	3	4	Score
Criteria 1	Description of characteristics of the work reflecting a low level of performance in the criteria.	Description of characteristics of the work reflecting an intermediate level of performance in the criteria.	Description of characteristics of the work reflecting a high level of performance in the criteria.	Description of characteristics of the work reflecting the highest level of performance in the criteria.	
Criteria 2	...	...	...	...	

Here's an example of a rubric to assess the activity *My favorite artist* in *Module 5, Being a musician*, where students have to create a photo story of their favorite artist. Level 1 in Criteria 1 (Use of images) might define the lowest level of performance as "The pictures are unrelated to the content and don't enhance understanding of the content, or are distracting and create a busy feeling", contrasting with level 4 which might be defined as "The images help in presenting an overall theme with a high impact message that appeals to the audience, demonstrating an excellent synthesis".

The full range is shown in the following table:

Criteria/ Level	1	2	3	4	Score
Use of images	The pictures are unrelated to the content and don't enhance understanding of the content, or are distracting and create a busy feeling.	Description of characteristics of the work reflecting an intermediate level of performance in the criteria.	Description of characteristics of the work reflecting a high level of performance in the criteria.	The images help in presenting an overall theme with a high impact message that appeals to the audience, demonstrating an excellent synthesis.	

Now, how do we score a work from a rubric? We just need to score it according to the several criteria that we have considered, according to the level of performance, and then apply a simple formula:

$$\text{Final classification} = \frac{\text{Total score} \times \text{the scale in which we want the final classification}}{\text{number of levels to be} \times \text{the number of criteria considered} \quad \text{used in the rubric}}$$

Here is an example:

We want to assess a work that is being scored in five criteria, each one with four levels of possible performances, and we want the final result in a scale of 0 to 100.

Criteria	Score (1 to 4)
Criteria 1	2
Criteria 2	3
Criteria 3	3
Criteria 4	4
Criteria 5	2
Total Score	**14**

So the final classification will be:

$$\text{Final classification} = \frac{(14 \times 100)}{(4 \times 5)} = 70$$

Criteria

Here is a list of criteria that can be useful when assessing multimedia works:

- Design
- Content
- Organization
- Navigation
- Technical aspects (such as lighting, pace, timing, exposure, color scheme, video continuity, and formats)
- Links (for example, in mind maps)
- Referencing
- Collaboration/Teamwork

Using an online spreadsheet such as Google Spreadsheets can be a good way of keeping records of our students' assessments according to these rubrics. We can obtain the final scores easily by applying formulas to cells, and can later publish them on the course page or by using Moodle's Gradebook. As this tool allows collaboration, if we have students as editors, they can also perform verification work and/or peer assessments.

Summary

In this chapter we looked at integrating multimedia elements into assessment activities in Moodle, such as quizzes, lessons, and assignments and how to add multiple choice multimedia answers to quizzes and lessons. We also considered two applications, Hot Potatoes and JClic, both of which are capable of not only producing different types of exercises such as crosswords or image puzzles, but also of facilitating the construction of quizzes. The activities created with these applications were later integrated in Moodle, in the first case using a dedicated activity into Moodle, and in the second by linking to the HTML file generated by JClic. Finally, we considered rubrics as an easy way of assessing multimedia works, considering some criteria that can be used to perform this task either by teachers or students. And as the assessment is already done, we are very close to the end. Let's now look at synchronous communication and interaction, learning how to communicate in real-time using text, audio and video, and creating an online classroom.

7
Synchronous Communication and Interaction

In this chapter, we will see how we can interact with our students in real time, specifically by using an online chat service and a desktop sharing application. These can be helpful for distance education, providing new ways of communicating and interacting with our students (and between them) when we are not all in the same physical space. Because Moodle does not provide effective synchronous communication tools (the chat activity could overload the server), the aforementioned tools are presented as extensions that can support our courses giving them a new level of interaction. In distance courses with considerable duration, such communication can be a motivation and a way of providing support to students when we are online at the same time.

By the end of this chapter you will be able to do the following:

- Using text, audio, video chat, and conferencing to support communication and collaboration in Moodle courses
- Sharing your desktop, a collaborative sketchpad, and files with students, supporting distance interaction in real time in Moodle courses
- Using a remote desktop functionality

Communicating in real time using text, audio, and video

Google+ Hangouts (`http://www.google.com/hangouts/`) is a service from Google that allows text, audio, and video chat among Google users. This means that we need a Google account, something that we have seen by now.

With this tool we can do the following:

- Meeting with colleagues or students, individually or in groups
- Participating in a distant event (for example, attending a conference)
- Conducting interviews
- Teaching how to play an instrument (by using the webcam)
- Teaching gestural language (by using the webcam)

I find it really useful to use a tool like this in distance courses not only to give feedback to students and get to know them better, but also to create opportunities for students to interact with each other during group tasks outside of these tutor-students meeting times.

A good time to use this application is in *Module 10, What's good music?* — a theme that fits well with an online debate about how to define quality criteria for music. Students will be required to work in groups and debate on what they think is good music and how it can be assessed.

Chat and group chat

The chat option is available either on our Gmail account or in Google+ Hangouts on the right sidebar in Google +. Audio and video hangouts require some extra setup; so don't worry about those for now, we'll cover that later.

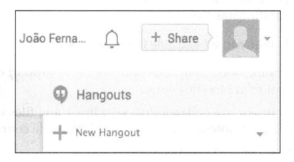

We are now ready to start a chat. We can search for contacts using the search form and double-click on the name of the contact that is displayed, or in the Hangout icon of the pop-up window that is displayed.

If we need a synchronous chat, it's obvious that the (two or more) people chatting must be online. However, we can also send messages if the person is not online, and he or she will receive them when online. We can check if a person is online or not by looking at the bar below the photo of the person in the contacts list. If they have a gray one, they are offline (or invisible and don't want to be bothered). If the color is green (available), yellow (idle), or red (busy), it's possible to chat with them.

After starting the chat, a window similar to the one shown in the following screenshot opens in the lower-right corner of the Google+ or Gmail account, and we can start talking:

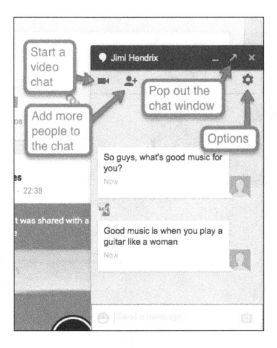

When we are chatting with someone, we can click on the Create a group Hangout icon to add more people to the chat.

Note that if we click on the arrow in the top bar of our chat window, it will pop out from its position so that we can access it as an independent window.

 If we paste a URL from a YouTube video into the chat window, a preview of the video will be integrated directly into our conversation, as shown in the following screenshot:

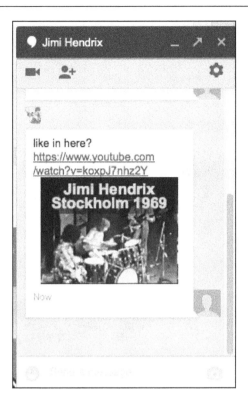

Voice and video chat

Chat, as we saw, is available by default in Google Mail and Google+. To add audio and voice capabilities to this chat, we have to install a plugin that is available at `https://www.google.com/tools/dlpage/hangoutplugin` for Windows and Mac users (again, sorry to Linux users).

After installing this plugin, we can start a voice or video conversation. If our contacts have a camera and microphone, we just need to click on the Video call icon on the top bar of the Hangout window.

A new Google+ Hangouts on Air window will pop-up, and a video of us and the person that we are chatting with will be displayed in the lower region of the window.

If we just want a voice call, we should click on the Turn camera off icon on the top right.

Creating an online real-time classroom

Google+ Hangouts on Air has several other functionalities that can be useful for online classrooms.

With a tool like this we can do the following:

- Demonstrating how to use a particular software
- Making online presentations to the entire class with real-time annotations using Microsoft PowerPoint, PDF files, or by sharing our entire desktop
- Drawing and commenting on a collaborative sketchpad

In our course, we could use this in several modules but it would fit well in *Module 4, Music as a language*. In this module, students have to create basic rhythms, harmonies, and melodies using free software, so that as a teacher we can discuss some of the basic music theory and use of applications to create music and sharing our desktop, in particular by using applications such as Finale Notepad or Hydrogen.

As we saw previously when we start a video call, we automatically start a Google+ Hangout on Air. As we have seen in *Chapter 4*, *Video*, in creating an online TV, this tool allows us to share our screen, remote desktop, or even share documents using Google Drive (and this can be used for a collaborative sketchpad too). Let's start with the **Screenshare** functionality.

Screenshare

The Screenshare app allows us to share our screen with all the participants of the Hangout. It's very handy in an online classroom if we want everyone to follow something we are watching or doing in our computer.

If we click on the **Screenshare** option, we are required to choose the window we want to share from all the windows we have opened in our computer.

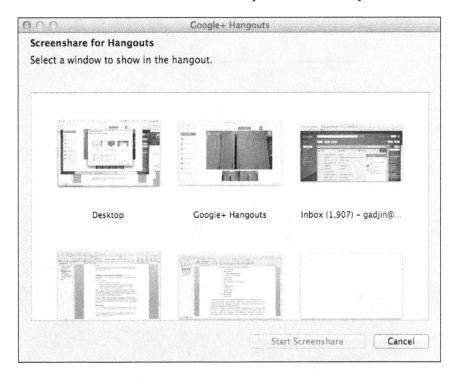

After we select the window to show in the Hangout, we just need to hit the **Start Screenshare** button.

Remote Desktop

The Remote Desktop app allows us to control the computer of one of the participants in the Hangout.

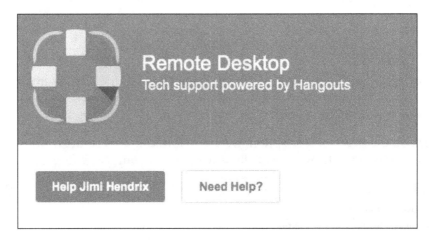

If we click on the Help "Participant" button (in our case, **Help Jimi Hendrix**), that participant will receive an invitation to accept our remote desktop request. After accepting it, we can control his/her computer.

The collaborative sketchpad

With the Google Drive app we can draw on a sketchpad with all the participants. The first thing to do is to install the app by navigating to **View more apps** | **Add apps** from the left menu and then searching for it in the available apps.

When the app is installed, after we click on it we are presented with the following screen:

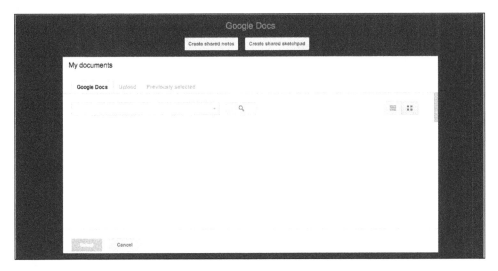

If we click on the **Create shared sketchpad** button, a shared drawing is opened and everyone can draw on it.

We can draw with a set of tools that are available at the top bar. These allow us to write, draw, insert images and shapes, and so on.

Sharing files

In the Google Drive app we can also create shared notes or upload documents, for example, a Microsoft PowerPoint presentation or an Adobe PDF, and discuss it while everyone is looking at it.

For that, we just need to click on the **Upload** tab and follow the instructions to send a file that is available to everyone on the Hangout.

Recording

Google+ Hangouts on Air has a default record functionality that keeps a copy of the meeting. This can also be a way of recording performances that students might be shy to perform directly in front of their peers or to help them in practicing for important tasks, for example, an interview. These recordings can be made available in Moodle for later discussion and commenting with a simple link.

Moodle it!

We can easily embed the live player of our Hangout On Air in Moodle. Once we're in the Hangout On Air, we just need to click on **Embed** and copy the YouTube URL or HTML code. Once the Hangout On Air is embedded, students can watch it directly from our course.

Summary

In this chapter, we have seen two ways of adding real-time communication and interaction to our Moodle course, firstly, by using Google+ Hangouts and secondly, by using Google+ Hangouts on Air. This interaction can be very useful, particularly for allowing students to communicate with each other and the teacher. For distance education, synchronous tools solve several problems that come from students being in different locations, allowing us to share desktops, presentations, sketchpads, voice, and video.

In the next chapter, we will finally conclude this book with some general aspects on copyright, licensing, safety related to multimedia works, and online collaboration.

8
Common Multimedia Issues in Moodle

In this chapter, we will discuss some common issues in using the several kinds of multimedia elements that we have discussed so far in our courses. In particular, this chapter considers the following:

- Copyright issues and referring to sources
- Internet safety (as our students will be using web-based tools in broader communities, and this has risks)
- Some issues with regard to web-based applications such as backups
- Some Moodle modules and plugins that can be interesting if we want to extend Moodle's multimedia capabilities

Copyright and licensing issues

While using multimedia works that have been created by others and that are not licensed under a Creative Commons or similar license (a license in which the author grants others the right to use the work under certain conditions), we should assume that the work is an **All rights reserved** creative work. This means that almost all use of it is protected by law (for example, for the United Kingdom, refer to `http://www.copyrightservice.co.uk/copyright` and for the United States of America, refer to `http://www.copyright.com/content/cc3/en/toolbar/education/get-the-facts.html`), and only the copyright author is allowed to make copies, distribute, translate, adapt, and perform other transformative uses for the works. However, there are some limited uses that the law allows that fit under the "fair use" umbrella. And if the work is old enough or the author has waived his rights, the work is in the public domain that is another kind of status, which means that there are no restrictions in using it. Let's see what these two concepts mean.

Using copyrighted work fairly

Fair use of a copyrighted work consists of using it for a limited and transformative purpose. This doesn't mean that we can make copies of an entire book or code and give it to our students because we are teaching and we have an excuse (that doesn't sound fair, does it?). So, there are some aspects to keep in mind that limit this label of fair use:

- The purpose and character of our use of the work – if it is to comment, criticize, parody, news report, or teach, we can use it

- The nature of the copyrighted work – if it is a highly-creative work or just factual, there will be more stringent limitations on the use of the work

- The amount and substantiality of the portion of the work taken by us – if we are using an acceptable sample of the work, this will not put at risk interest in the entire work (a 10 percent rule usually applies to fair use)

- The effect of our use of the work upon the potential market – if it loses market share due to our use of it, it's not fair use

These guidelines give room for interpretation (refer to `http://fairuse.stanford.edu/overview/fair-use/four-factors/`), but if we keep them in mind, (for example, just use short clips from a video, something like 10 percent, and keep it private in your Moodle course and do not publish it, for example, on YouTube), it will almost certainly qualify as fair use. I can't personally guarantee this because I'm not a judge; I just know these guidelines and follow my common sense. For example, because the course *Music for everyday life* is freely accessible on the Web, I avoided using copyrighted works in this way. There are copyright charts produced by several organizations with more specific guidelines, such as `http://www.halldavidson.net/copyright_chart.pdf`, that can be helpful. Also, watch the videos *Copyright: Forever Less One Day* at `http://www.youtube.com/watch?v=tk862BbjWx4` and *A Fair(y) Use Tale* at `http://www.youtube.com/watch?v=CJn_jC4FNDo` about this issue.

Bear in mind that we can always ask the copyright owner if we can use his or her work in a specific context. This can take time but if we really want to use a substantial part of the work, this is the safest way to do it.

This is something that we can discuss with our students, as they too will be using other people's works to make their own. This can raise issues of social justice, the nature of creativity as an incremental process, and why some things should be free no matter what.

Using works in the public domain

We can use any work that is in the public domain without obtaining the permission of the original author or copyright owner. A work qualifies as being in the public domain when the following conditions are satisfied:

- The copyright term has expired or the copyright protection for that work was not maintained in a manner that was essential

- The work is an unpublished work and special rules indicate that it has fallen into the public domain

- The author or copyright owner has dedicated the work to the public domain

We can find works in the public domain in Wikimedia Commons (`http://commons.wikimedia.org`) and the Internet Archive (`http://www.archive.org`). All of the classical music before the 19th century is in the public domain, and all of the works published in the United States before 1928 (as of 2013) also qualify. In one of the activities in our course that we saw in *Chapter 3, Sound and Music*, classical music examples that fitted this categorization were used.

There is a nice comic book about these two concepts, *Tales from the Public Domain: BOUND BY LAW*, that you should take a look at.

Source: Aoki, K., Boyle, J. & Jenkins, J. (2006). Bound by law?. Retrieved on February 17, 2009 from http://www.law.duke.edu/cspd/comics

Licensing your work under a Creative Commons license

Creative Commons (http://creativecommons.org) is a nonprofit corporation whose mission is to make it easier for people to share and build upon the work of others. For this, it has created a set of licenses that provide authors with standardized permissions that they can attach to their digital works, informing users of the author's work on what they can and cannot do with this work.

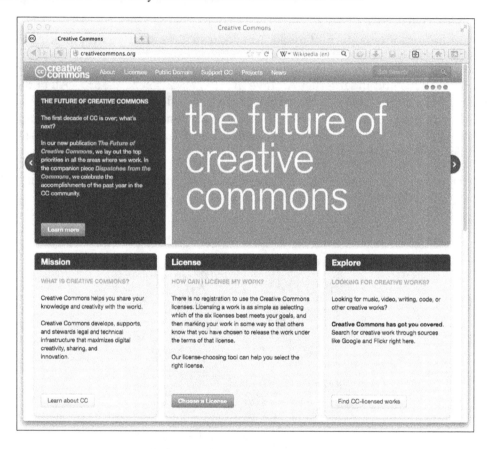

With the possibilities of digital media, it's easier for everyone to remix and create something new from the work of others. If we depended on author permissions or fair use rules, the process would be slower (as we saw, if no license is associated to a work, we have to assume that a work is an All rights reserved work, with all of the restrictions inherent to this). Creative Commons is a way of accelerating the process.

Creative Commons licenses are used quite a lot on the Web today, being applied to blogs, websites, photos, or videos, just to name a few examples.

There are four permissions that are contained in Creative Commons licenses:

- **Attribution (BY)**: This requires users to attribute a work to its original author. This covers all of the licenses
- **Attribution-ShareAlike (SA)**: This is a copyleft requirement that requires that any derived works be licensed under the same license
- **Attribution-NoDerivs (ND)**: This license is used by authors where they restrict modification
- **Attribution-NonCommercial (NC)**: This requires that the work is not used for commercial purposes

So we can license, for example, a worksheet that we created for a class with an Attribution-NonCommercial license, which would only restrict the sale of this worksheet if a profit is involved. We would, in this case, attach the logo for this particular license to the work, as shown in the following screenshot:

We should also add a link to the license, for example, `http://creativecommons.org/licenses/by-nc/3.0`.

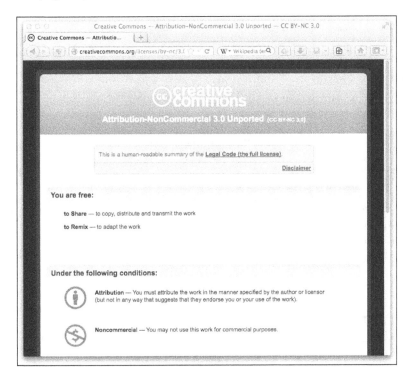

The course *Music for everyday life* was licensed in this way using a **Creative Commons Attribution 3.0** license. You will notice the logo and link in the footer of the course.

To select a Creative Commons license for our work (this also means our students), we can go to http://creativecommons.org/choose and create the license that we want to use, and then add the license to the multimedia work (for example, either in the page where our work will be made available or at the end of a movie).

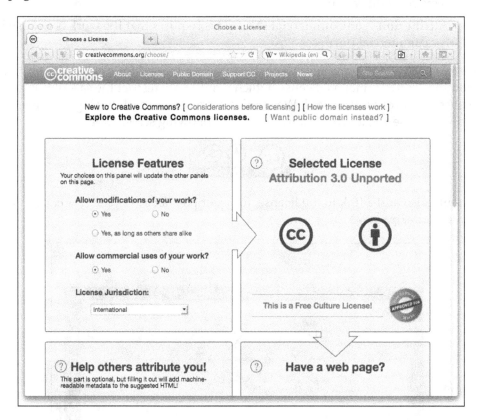

Again, bear in mind that if we don't attach any license to our works, this means it will be considered by law as an All rights reserved work. In this case, we might want to add our contact information to the work so that others can contact us and ask for specific permissions to re-use it.

There are other licenses that we can use while making our works available for others to build upon, such as the **GNU Free Documentation License**—a license by the **Free Software Foundation**, as used in Wikipedia. This is a copyleft license, meaning that derivative works should keep the same license. The **GPL** (**General Public License**) has the same concept, but specifically applies to software.

Referencing sources

In a digital world, referencing the sources that we use in our works is fundamental not just from an ethical perspective but also to inform others of where we found the sources, so that they can find them easily too and use them if they wish. In a way, a reference is a link and can be used to find something that we found interesting or inspiring.

There are several ways to reference a source using different standards defined by institutions such as the **APA (American Psychological Association)**. To cite a podcast, for example, made by me and my editors about writing a book without burning out, that was made available at `http://musicforeverydaylife.net` on Sept 1 and accessed the next day on the same web page, I would write the following reference:

Fenandes, J., Dewani, R., Dixit, R., Khambatta, R., and *Nair, A.* (Feb 1, 2013). *Writing a book without burning out – tips and techniques.* Retrieved Sept 2, 2013, from `http://musicforeverydaylife.net`.

Understanding plagiarism

Plagiarism can become hard to detect in multimedia content. Previously, in exclusively textual works, we could copy an excerpt of the work and Google it to see if there were similar texts on the Web. With music, voice, or video, this can't be done so easily (tags can help, though) and as much as the activities that we design for our students are meaningful and extremely interesting, deadlines can lead to students plagiarizing other people's work. Discussing this from time to time, communicating expectations, making consequences clear, encouraging oral presentations of their work, and questioning them on how they developed their ideas can minimize this.

Seeking further advice

There are some places to go and ask for further advice on copyright issues:

- The librarian at our school, university, or community can usually help
- The LSE's *Short Guide to Copyright for Staff* is available at `http://www.lse.ac.uk/library/services/liaison/ShortGuideToCopyright.aspx`
- The *APA Referencing Guide* by Waikato University, New Zealand is available at `http://www.waikato.ac.nz/library/study/guides/apa.shtml`
- *The Code of Best Practices in Fair Use for Media Literacy Education* is available at `http://www.centerforsocialmedia.org/resources/publications/code_for_media_literacy_education`

Understanding safety issues

As we use the Web, especially while using online communities to post some of our multimedia works, there are some safety issues to keep in mind and we should *always* inform our students about these. This can be done during class and reinforced by a school's policy (an acceptable usage policy, which can be connected to other policies on certain issues such as bullying or plagiarism). Some safety issues that we should be aware of are listed here.

Personal details

Personal details are sensitive information that can be used by people with bad intentions to establish contact with people, bully them, or even to steal online identities. Depending on their age, our students should keep their details to a minimum (no online usernames, no mobile phone numbers, and so on) while creating accounts in online communities, should avoid publishing photos of themselves and their colleagues without their parents' permission, and should never arrange meetings with strangers through the Web.

Cyber bullying

Sometimes, the Web can be used to intimidate or threaten people. It might happen that in a community in Moodle or through e-mail, colleagues or others bully one of our students using threatening messages. We can only prevent this by discussing ethical issues with our students and by being aware of changes in behavior or students' comments, working with parents to solve this. For parents, a good practice is to place the computer that is connected to the Web at home in a shared area, and to engage in conversations about their children's activities on the Web (and to participate in them). Often, schools now create a parent's login so that they can see what their children are doing in Moodle.

Seeking further advice

There are some websites and organizations that can help us to address e-safety with our students, providing interesting resources and training such as:

- Insafe (http://www.saferinternet.org)
- The thinkuknow website (http://www.thinkuknow.co.uk), which is published by the Child Exploitation and Online Protection (CEOP) Centre
- WISE KIDS (http://www.wisekids.org.uk)
- Childnet International (http://www.childnet-int.org)

Selecting web-based applications

While selecting web-based applications to use in our courses, there are some issues that we should be aware of. We already saw some privacy and safety aspects of this, so now let's have a look at some other aspects of it.

- **Ownership and licensing**: The ownership of the works that we make available online should remain ours. With regard to licensing, the company that manages the web application has the right to distribute our work (of course, this makes sense). The license that we provide to them shouldn't be too unrestricted, though. Always check the **Terms of Service** for this. There should also be tools to enable us, as authors, to attach a license to our works (as is the case with Flickr).

- **Formats**: Services that use PNG, JPEG, Flash Video, MPEG-4, MP3, and all of the open web standards should be acceptable (HTML, XML, and RSS).

- **Offline backup**: All the services should have a backup facility, or facilitate this in some way, especially if editing is performed online (as is the case with online video subtitling). If it's about sending our own files, we should always keep a copy on our computer or another media.

- **The level of activity of the community and development team**: High levels of participation both from the participants of the community and the development team (for example, check the company's blogs) is usually a good sign. And of course, a larger community exponentially increases the number of potential relationships.

Never forget to read the Terms of Service of a web application or community before joining it. This is particularly true while working with students, as some applications and communities can also have age restrictions attached to them.

Moodle plugins of interest

At `http://moodle.org/plugins`, we can find many plugins submitted by developers from around the world. Because this is a book about Moodle and multimedia, here is a short list of modules and plugins relating to multimedia:

- **Poodll**: This plugin allows us to put widgets such as stopwatches and flashcards into HTML areas. You can get this plugin from `https://moodle.org/plugins/view.php?plugin=filter_poodll`.

- **Streaming media filter (RTMP)**: This plugin allows us to embed video streamings using the RTMP protocol. You can get this plugin from `https://moodle.org/plugins/view.php?plugin=filter_rtmp`.

- **Geogebra**: This plugin is a filter that allows us to add any model made with the Geogebra geometry application available at `http://www.geogebra.org`. You can get this plugin from `https://moodle.org/plugins/view.php?plugin=mod_geogebra`.

- **EJSApp**: This plugin allows us to add any applet made with Easy Java Simulations. You can get this plugin from `https://moodle.org/plugins/view.php?plugin=mod_ejsapp`.

Summary

In this final chapter, we looked at copyright issues while using digital works created by others, analyzing some uses that fit under the fair use umbrella, which is of most interest to teachers and trainers. We also learned about other kinds of licenses, such as Creative Commons licenses, that don't just describe allowed uses of the author of a work but also provide a way of licensing our multimedia works on the Web. We learned how to reference the sources that we use in our creations by using the APA style guide, which is one of many styles available for doing this. Not least, we considered some safety issues while having our students involved in and exposed to larger web communities, and examined some criteria for selecting web-based applications to use and communities to be part of. Finally, we looked at some plugins that have been developed by Moodle developers and that can help us integrate Moodle multimedia elements.

After all of these pages, we've finally come to the end of this book. I hope you have found it useful for introducing multimedia in your Moodle courses, and most of all, I hope this new way of doing things brings performance, not just for your teaching but particularly for your students' learning. Without this, any effort or innovation is nonsense.

This book was written around a very simple idea — we, teachers, trainers, and most of all, students with free and accessible tools and some basic know-how, can create simple multimedia elements and tasks easily and integrate them in Moodle for learning in our everyday lives. I hope you find this idea useful and more than that, effective. And by using multimedia in Moodle not just as a product for better delivery, but also to improve the ways in which students can construct, you can bring more imagination and learning to your classes.

Index

R

Record button 104
Remote Desktop app 228
room
  creating, Floor planner used 159, 160
Rotate button 52
Rotate tool 52
rubrics
  used, for multimedia assessing 218, 220
rule of thirds 41

S

safety issues
  about 240
  cyber bullying 240
  e-safety references 240
  personal details 240
Save changes button 37, 73
Save & Continue button 111
Save image as... option 27
Scale button 49
screencast, creating with Google Hangouts
  about 145
  screen recording, with audio 146
  stop motion movie, creating with JellyCam
    146, 147
Screenshare app 227
screenshots
  capturing 61
  capturing, GIMP used 61-63
  capturing, Jing used 64, 65
See more link 25
Selection tool 100
Select some files button 111
Sequences tab 215
Share button 154
shared folder
  creating, Google Drive used 155, 156
Share... option 156
Share&Promote tab 69
Share & save button 154
Show Onion Skin tool 147
Site administration block 15, 16
SlideShare
  URL 72
  used, for presentations publishing 72, 73

slideshows
  creating 70-78
  online photo slideshows, creating 74-78
  PowerPoint slides, exporting to build
    Moodle lessons 70, 71
  SlideShare used, for presentations
    publishing 72, 73
Slide size options button 70
sound
  adding, to forums 18, 19
  using, in forums 19
Soundbible
  URL 83
Soundtrackers activity 46, 48, 51
Spaces for music theme 12
START BROADCAST button 141
Start Broadcasting button 145
Start tab 151
Stock.XCHNG
  about 31
  URL 31
story
  adding, in interactive timelines 172
Story media tab 173
Stripgenerator
  about 66
  URL 66
  used, for comic strips creating 66-69
Student role 15

T

TED Talks
  URL 117
text to speech
  conversion, Voki used 106, 107
  used, for voice assignment 108, 109
Themes tab 70
The science of music theme 12
Tiki-Toki
  URL 171
  used, for interactive timelines creating 170,
    172
timeline 98
Time shift tool 105
titles
  adding 137

Thank you for buying
Moodle 2.5 Multimedia

About Packt Publishing

Packt, pronounced 'packed', published its first book "*Mastering phpMyAdmin for Effective MySQL Management*" in April 2004 and subsequently continued to specialize in publishing highly focused books on specific technologies and solutions.

Our books and publications share the experiences of your fellow IT professionals in adapting and customizing today's systems, applications, and frameworks. Our solution based books give you the knowledge and power to customize the software and technologies you're using to get the job done. Packt books are more specific and less general than the IT books you have seen in the past. Our unique business model allows us to bring you more focused information, giving you more of what you need to know, and less of what you don't.

Packt is a modern, yet unique publishing company, which focuses on producing quality, cutting-edge books for communities of developers, administrators, and newbies alike. For more information, please visit our website: www.packtpub.com.

About Packt Open Source

In 2010, Packt launched two new brands, Packt Open Source and Packt Enterprise, in order to continue its focus on specialization. This book is part of the Packt Open Source brand, home to books published on software built around Open Source licences, and offering information to anybody from advanced developers to budding web designers. The Open Source brand also runs Packt's Open Source Royalty Scheme, by which Packt gives a royalty to each Open Source project about whose software a book is sold.

Writing for Packt

We welcome all inquiries from people who are interested in authoring. Book proposals should be sent to author@packtpub.com. If your book idea is still at an early stage and you would like to discuss it first before writing a formal book proposal, contact us; one of our commissioning editors will get in touch with you.

We're not just looking for published authors; if you have strong technical skills but no writing experience, our experienced editors can help you develop a writing career, or simply get some additional reward for your expertise.

Moodle 2.5 Multimedia Cookbook
Second Edition

ISBN: 978-1-78328-937-0   Paperback: 300 pages

75 recipes to help you integrate different multimedia resources into your Moodle courses to make them more interactive

1. Add all sorts of multimedia features to your Moodle course

2. Lots of easy-to-follow, step-by-step recipes

3. Work with sound, audio, and animation to make your course even more interactive

---

Moodle Gradebook

ISBN: 978-1-84951-814-7   Paperback: 128 pages

Set up and customize the gradebook to track student progress through Moodle

1. Use Moodle's powerful gradebook more effectively to monitor and report the progress of your students

2. Customize the gradebook to calculate and show the information you need

3. Discover new grading features and tracking functions now available in Moodle 2

Please check **www.PacktPub.com** for information on our titles

Moodle for Mobile Learning

ISBN: 978-1-78216-438-8   Paperback: 234 pages

Connect, communicate, and promote collaboration with your coursework using Moodle

1. Adopts practical ideas for demonstrating how to implement mobile learning with Moodle

2. Empowers you to apply mobile learning in your profession

3. Discover how other organizations have achieved mobile learning success

4. Filled with practical and hands-on tutorials for learning practitioners

Moodle 2 for Teaching 7-14 Year Olds Beginner's Guide

ISBN: 978-1-84951-832-1   Paperback: 258 pages

Effective e-learning for younger students, using Moodle as your classroom assistant

1. Ideal for teachers new to Moodle: easy to follow and abundantly illustrated with screenshots of the solutions you'll build

2. Go paperless! Put your lessons online and grade them anywhere, anytime

3. Engage and motivate your students with games, quizzes, movies, blogs, and podcasts the whole class can participate in

Please check **www.PacktPub.com** for information on our titles

www.ingramcontent.com/pod-product-compliance
Lightning Source LLC
Chambersburg PA
CBHW060532060326
40690CB00017B/3464